quiltstyle
cool and cozy coverlets

Tammy Tadd

CREATIVE Home
HOMEOWNER® Arts

CRE▲TIVE
HOMEOWNER®

A Division of Federal Marketing Corp.
Upper Saddle River, NJ

❋ QUILT STYLE is designed to make "hands-free" crafting possible. Stand up this book with the steps of the desired project facing you. Follow the steps as directed. When it comes time to go to the next page of directions, flip the page over, and the next steps will face you.

❋ Stand up the book and read here first.

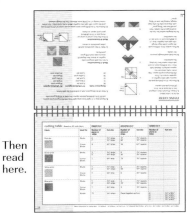

❋ Then read here.

QUILT STYLE: COOL AND COZY COVERLETS

SENIOR EDITOR:	Carol Endler Sterbenz
SENIOR DESIGNER:	Glee Barre
EDITORIAL ASSISTANTS:	Jennifer Calvert
	Nora Grace
PHOTO RESEARCHER:	Robyn Poplasky
TECHNICAL EDITOR:	Amy O'Neill Houck
ASSISTANT DESIGNER:	Amanda Wilson
DIAGRAMS:	Tammy Tadd
COVER DESIGN:	Glee Barre
INDEXER:	Schroeder Indexing Services
PRINCIPAL PHOTOGRAPHER:	Steven Mays
INSTRUCTIONAL PHOTOGRAPHER:	Dennis Johnson
PHOTO STYLIST:	Genevieve A. Sterbenz

CREATIVE HOMEOWNER

VP / EDITORIAL DIRECTOR:	Timothy O. Bakke
PRODUCTION MANAGER:	Kimberly H. Vivas
ART DIRECTOR:	David Geer
MANAGING EDITOR:	Fran J. Donegan

Current Printing (last digit)
10 9 8 7 6 5 4 3 2 1

Quilt Style: Cool and Cozy Coverlets, First Edition
Library of Congress Control Number: 2006931869
ISBN-10: 1-58011-332-X
ISBN-13: 978-1-58011-332-8

CREATIVE HOMEOWNER®
A Division of Federal Marketing Corp.
24 Park Way
Upper Saddle River, NJ 07458
www.creativehomeowner.com

dedication

To Velda, my mom and my biggest fan, who has believed in me from the beginning. And to my husband, Gary, and my children, Olivia, Stephanie, Nicholas, Haley, and Garrison, for your never-ending support and encouragement.

table of contents

introducing the collection

The excitement builds as you walk through the front door of the local quilt shop and head toward your favorite area of the store. The warm tones of carmel or burgundy might draw you forward. Or maybe the softer, paler palettes will appeal more to you. These personal preferences will help you to develop your own "quilt style."

As you look through the pages of **QUILT STYLE: Cool and Cozy Coverlets,** some quilts may catch your eye right away. Envision each project with a twist of your own style. Choose to make a project shown in "the collection" or one of the color variations pictured. Let your own

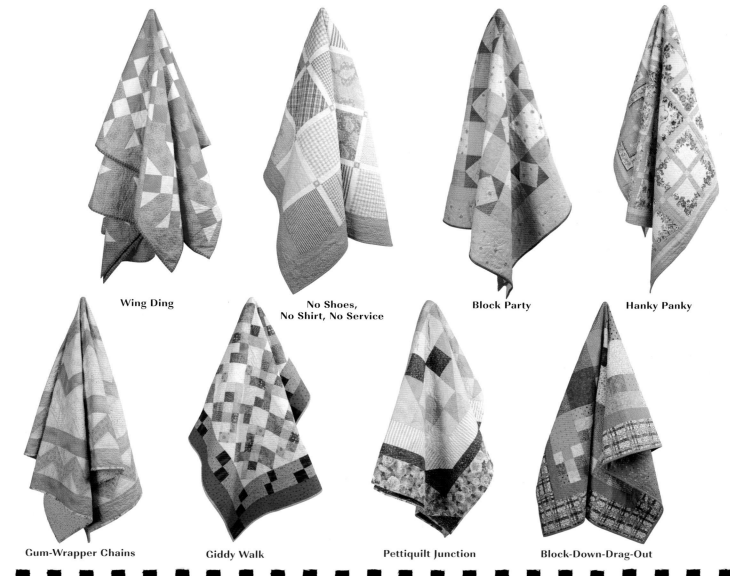

Wing Ding

No Shoes,
No Shirt, No Service

Block Party

Hanky Panky

Gum-Wrapper Chains

Giddy Walk

Pettiquilt Junction

Block-Down-Drag-Out

personal style shine through.

Whether you consider yourself an expert quilter or just a beginner, **QUILT STYLE** has something for you. From quick and simple designs to more time-consuming, involved quilts, you can work your way through every project and experience a great sense of accomplishment with each one. Enjoy perfecting the art of quilting.

My hope is that you find that this book—and every beautiful quilt you make— brings you great joy and helps you discover the "quilt style" that truly makes you happy.

Tammy Dadd

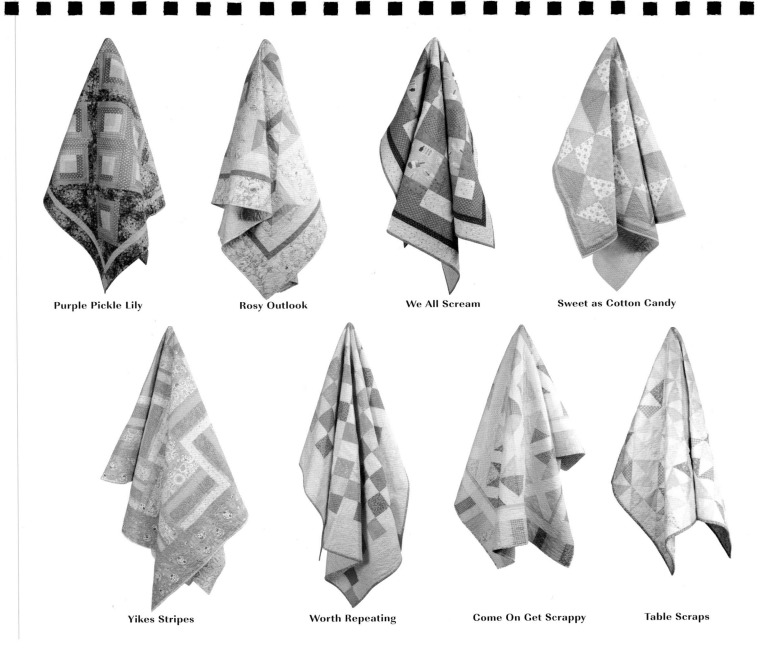

Purple Pickle Lily   **Rosy Outlook**   **We All Scream**   **Sweet as Cotton Candy**

Yikes Stripes   **Worth Repeating**   **Come On Get Scrappy**   **Table Scraps**

gum-wrapper chains

"flying geese" recast

Here, a quilt whose strikingly graphic design is based on the traditional quilt pattern "flying geese" is recast in a nostalgic light. If you were a teenage girl back in the '60s and '70s, you might remember folding and weaving paper gum wrappers into a "chain." The shape of the chain resembles the "flying geese" pattern in the featured quilt. Even if you have never made a chain out of gum wrappers, you will enjoy making this quilt from pieces of pretty fabrics in green, yellow, and blue prints. When the zigzag of the pattern is set against the pink fabric, the quilt appears to be divided into triangles.

skill level
Intermediate

throw size
60" x 72" (1.52m x 1.83m)

block size
6" (15.24cm)

yardages
- 2 ¼ yds. (2.06m) pink-dot fabric
- 1 yd. (0.91m) green-print fabric
- ⅝ yd. (0.57m) yellow-print fabric
- 1 ¾ yds. (1.60m) blue-print fabric
- 3 ¾ yds. (3.43m) backing fabric, as desired
- 66" x 78" (1.68m x 1.98m) batting
- ½ yd. (0.46m) binding fabric, as desired

Quilt made by Sharon Olson, machine-quilted by Sherry Massey

cutting table — Based on 42"-wide fabric

Fabric	Used for	FIRST CUT Number of pieces or strips	FIRST CUT Cut size	SECOND CUT Number of pieces or strips	SECOND CUT Cut size	THIRD CUT Number of pieces or strips	THIRD CUT Cut size
Pink-dot	Blocks	4	7¼" strips	17	7¼" squares		
		7	3⅞" strips	68	3⅞" squares		
	Corner blocks	3	6½" strips	16	6½" squares		
Green print 	Blocks	2	7¼" strips	9	7¼" squares		
		4	3⅞" strips	36	3⅞" squares		
	Corner blocks	1	3½" strip	12	3½" squares		
Yellow print 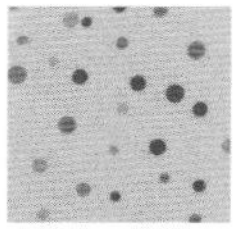	Blocks	1	7¼" strip	5	7¼" squares		
		2	3⅞" strips	20	3⅞" squares		
	Corner blocks	1	3½" strip	8	3½" squares		
Blue print 	Blocks	1	7¼" strip	3	7¼" squares		
		2	3⅞" strips	12	3⅞" squares		
	Corner blocks	1	3½" strip	4	3½" squares		
	Border	11	3½" strips	Piece together and cut		2	3½" x 36½"
						2	3½" x 48½"
						2	3½" x 54½"
						2	3½" x 66½"

Metric conversions for cutting table: 3½"(8.89cm)   3⅞"(9.84cm)   6½"(16.51cm)   7¼"(18.42cm)   36½"(0.93m)   42"(1.07m)   48½"(1.22m)   54½"(1.38m)   66½"(1.69m)

FLYING GEESE

BLOCK CONSTRUCTION

1. Using a #2 pencil, draw a diagonal line on the back of the 3⅞-in. (9.84cm) pink-dot squares.

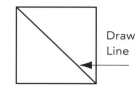

1

Draw Line

2. Place two 3⅞-in. (9.84cm) pink-dot squares, right sides together, in opposite corners of a 7¼-in. (18.42cm) green-print square. Clip in the center where the two squares overlap to eliminate bulk. Sew a ¼-in. (0.64cm) seam on each side of the marked line. Cut along the marked line.

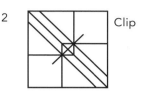

2

Clip

3. Iron both small triangle pieces to the outside.

3

4. Place another 3⅞-in. (9.84cm) pink-dot square on the large triangle with right sides together. Sew a ¼-in. (0.64cm) seam on each side of the marked line.

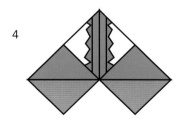

4

5. Cut along the marked line. Iron the small triangles to the outside. Note: you will have two "flying geese" units. Repeat to make the other large triangle, making four units of "flying geese."

5

6. Repeat steps 1–5 eight times using eight 7¼-in. (18.42cm) green-print squares and 32 3⅞-in. (9.84cm) pink-dot squares, for a total of 36 flying geese units.

7. Make all the flying geese units as indicated in the table below:

Flying Geese Units	7¼" (18.42cm) squares	3⅞" (9.84cm) squares
36	9 pink dot	36 green print
12	3 blue print	12 pink dot
12	3 pink dot	12 blue print
20	5 yellow print	20 pink dot
20	5 pink dot	20 yellow print

Block A Construction:

1. Sew two pink-and-green units together as shown. Iron. Repeat 35 times to make total of 36 green-print blocks.

2. Make 12 blue-print blocks and 20 yellow-print blocks as shown.

Block B Construction:

1. Draw line from corner to corner on wrong side of 3½-in. (8.89cm) green-print square, as shown.

2. Position the 3½-in. (8.89cm) green-print square on one corner of a 6½-in. (16.51cm) pink-dot square with right sides together. Stitch on the marked line. Trim off the corner, leaving a ¼-in. (0.64cm) seam allowance. Iron the triangle outward.

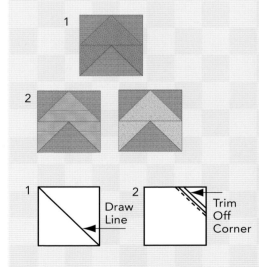

1

2

1 Draw Line

2 Trim Off Corner

COLOR VARIATION

Although the colors shown in this design are not my usual choices, they look beautiful when shown on a bed. The "flying geese" pattern shows off the zigzag design, highlighting the richness of the brown and blue fabrics.

Hint: for a more enjoyable quilting experience, be sure to take frequent breaks. Get up, and walk away from your work for a few minutes every hour or so. You will have a refreshed point of view when you return to your work.

3. Repeat steps 1–2 seven more times to make a total of eight pink-dot-and-green-print Block Bs.

4. Repeat the above steps replacing the 3½-in. (8.89cm) blue-print squares and 3½-in. (8.89cm) yellow-print squares for the 3½-in. (8.89cm) green-print squares to make four pink-dot-and-blue-print Block Bs and four pink-dot-and-yellow-print Block Bs.

QUILT TOP ASSEMBLY

1. Sew four yellow print Block As and two pink-dot and yellow-print Block Bs. Iron. Repeat once for rows #1 and #8.

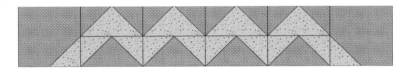

2. Sew two yellow-print Block As, two pink-dot-and-blue-print Block Bs and two blue-print Block As as shown. Press. Repeat once for rows #2 and #7.

3. Sew two yellow-print Block As, two blue-print Block As and two pink-dot-and-green-print Block Bs as shown. Iron. Repeat once for rows #3 and #6.

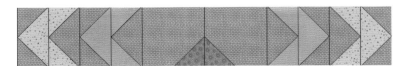

4. Sew two yellow-print Block As, two blue-print Block As and two green-print Block As as shown. Iron. Repeat once for rows #4 and #5.

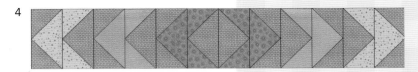

5. Sew together the eight rows just made to complete the quilt center. Iron.

Inner Framing

1. Sew one 3½-in. x 48½-in. (8.89cm x 1.23m) blue-print strip to each side of the quilt center. Iron.

2. Sew a 3½-in. (8.89cm) yellow-print square to each end of a 3½-in. x 36½-in. (8.89cm x 92.71cm) blue-print strip. Iron. Sew this strip to the top of the quilt center. Iron. Repeat to make and sew the bottom border.

Pieced Border

1. Sew nine green Block As together to make a border. Iron. Sew the border to one side of the quilt. Iron. Repeat to make and sew the other side border.

2. Sew seven green Block As together. Add a pink-dot-and-green-print Block B to each end of the border unit. Iron. Sew the border to the top of the quilt. Repeat to make and sew the bottom border.

Outer Border

1. Sew a 3½-in. x 66½-in. (8.89cm x 1.69m) blue-print strip to each side of the quilt. Iron.

2. Sew one 3½-in. (8.89cm) green-print square to each end of a 3½-in. x 54½-in. (8.89cm x 1.38m) blue-print strip. Iron. Sew the strip to the top of the quilt. Iron. Repeat to make and sew the bottom border.

FINISHING YOUR QUILT

1. Layer your quilt top, batting, and backing. Quilt as desired.

block party

welcoming and cheerful

The summer season is a time when friends and neighbors get together, sharing sunset dinners or entertaining out-of-town guests. "Block Party" is the perfect welcoming quilt, whether it is set down on a grassy bank for a leisurely picnic or laid over a pullout couch and stacked with plump pillows. Made in vivacious pink florals and light-green prints, the blocks that make up the quilt are a mix of sweet prints and colors that are attractively old-fashioned. When the blocks are sewn together, they combine to create a quilt that is surprisingly graphic and modern in style.

skill level
Easy/Intermediate

twin size
70" x 93" (1.78m x 2.36m)

block size
6" (15.24cm)

yardages
- 2 yds. (1.83m) pink floral print fabric
- 1⅛ yds. (1.03m) pink print fabric
- 1⅝ yds. (1.49m) lt.-green print fabric
- ½ yd. (0.46m) med.-green print fabric
- ¾ yd. (0.69m) white floral print fabric
- ¾ yd. (0.69m) dk.-pink print fabric
- 5½ yds. (5.03m) backing fabric, as desired
- 75" x 99" (1.91m x 2.51m) quilt batting
- ⅝ yd. (0.57m) binding fabric, as desired

Quilt made by Sharon Olson, machine-quilted by Sherry Massey

cutting table   Based on a 42"-wide fabric

Fabric	Used for	FIRST CUT Number of pieces or crosswise strips	FIRST CUT Cut size	SECOND CUT Number of pieces or crosswise strips	SECOND CUT Cut size	THIRD CUT Number of pieces or crosswise strips	THIRD CUT Cut size
Pink floral 	Block A	5	4¾" strips	35	4¾" squares		
	Border	8	5½" strips	Piece together and cut		2	5½" x 59½"
						2	5½" x 83½"
Pink print 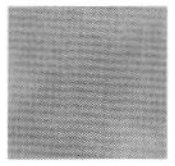	Block B	10	3½" strips				
Light-green print 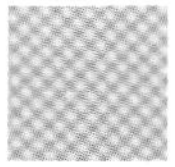	Block B	10	3½" strips			2	3" x 54½"
	Border	7	3" strips	Piece together and cut		2	3" x 78½"
Medium-green print 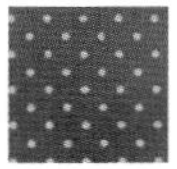	Block A	4	3⅞" strips	35	3⅞" squares	Cut in half once diagonally	
White floral 	Block	4	6½" strips	24	6½" squares		
Dark-pink print 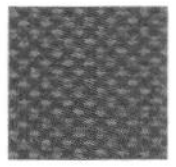	Corner blocks	1	5½" strip	4	5½" squares		
				4	3" squares		
	Block A	4	3⅞" strips	35	3⅞" squares	Cut in half once diagonally	

Metric conversions for cutting table: 3"(7.62cm)   3½" (8.89cm)   3⅞"(9.84cm)   4¾"(12.07cm)   5½"(13.97cm)   6½"(16.51cm)   42"(1.07m)   54½"(1.38cm)
59½"(1.51m)   78½"(1.99m)   83½"(2.12m)

BLOCK PARTY

BLOCK ASSEMBLY

Block A

1. Sew a 3⅞-in. (9.84cm) medium-green print triangle to the opposite sides of a 4¾-in. (12.07cm) pink floral square. Iron.

2. Sew a 3⅞-in. (9.84cm) dark-pink print triangle to the other two sides. Iron.

3. Repeat steps 1–2 34 times to make a total of 35 Block As.

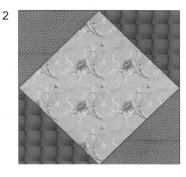

2

Block B

1. Sew a 3½-in. (8.89cm) pink-print strip and a 3½-in. (8.89cm) light-green-print strip together to make one strip set. Iron. Repeat nine times for a total of ten strip sets.

2. Cut the strip sets into 58 6½-in.-wide strip set segments.

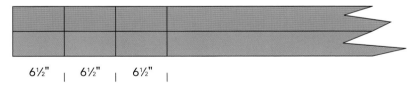

6½"   6½"   6½"

QUILT ASSEMBLY

Note: there are 13 columns, each composed of nine pieced squares.

1. Sew five Block As and four Block Bs together as shown in the diagram. Iron. Repeat three times to make a total of four columns (1, 5, 9, and 13).

2. Sew five Block Bs and four 6½-in.-wide (16.51cm) white floral squares together as shown. Iron. Repeat five times to make a total of six columns (2, 4, 6, 8, 10, and 12).

3. Sew five Block As and four Block Bs together as shown. Iron. Repeat two times to make a total of three columns (3, 7, and 11).

4. Referring to the "Whole Quilt Diagram" on page 19, sew together the 13 columns. Iron.

Quilts made in bright colors, especially in pinks and greens, evoke lush summer gardens filled with blooming flowers.

"It's not that quilting requires all night to accomplish, but there's something deeply reassuring about settling down to work after the house is quiet. It seems as though night suddenly dissolves into morning." Anonymous

COLOR VARIATION

A n ideal display of the overall effect that color change has on a project is this variation of "Block Party." The quilt pattern preserves its simplistic beauty, and the use of more traditional folk-art colors evokes the antique quilts that are still prized for their palette, ingenuity, and workmanship.

ADDING BORDERS

Inner Border

1. Sew a 3-in. x 78½-in. (7.62cm x 1.99m) light-green strip to each side of the quilt center. Iron.

2. Sew a 3-in. (7.62cm) dark-pink-print square on each end of a 3-in. x 54½-in. (7.62cm x 1.38m) light-green strip. Sew the strip to the top of the quilt center. Repeat at the bottom of the quilt to add the bottom border. Iron.

Outer Border

1. Sew a 5½-in. x 83½-in. (13.97cm x 2.12m) pink-floral strip to each side of the quilt center. Iron.

2. Sew a 5½-in. (13.97cm) dark-pink square to each end of a 5½-in. x 59½-in. (13.97cm x 1.51m) pink floral strip. Sew the strip to the top of the quilt. Repeat at the bottom of the quilt. Iron.

FINISHING YOUR QUILT

1. Layer your quilt top, batting, and backing. See "Layering the Quilt," on page 118. Quilt as desired.

TIP

To show off a beautiful quilt, lay it on a bed large enough to showcase the entire pattern. Or add a hanging sleeve to the back, and display it on a wall.

Bias Edges

"Block Party" calls for 3⅞-in. (9.84cm) squares that are cut in half diagonally across the bias (or the grain) of the fabric, creating two 3⅞-in. (9.84cm) triangles with bias edges. Bias edges can stretch out of shape, so handle them with care when sewing across the bias and when assembling the quilt.

Whole Quilt Diagram

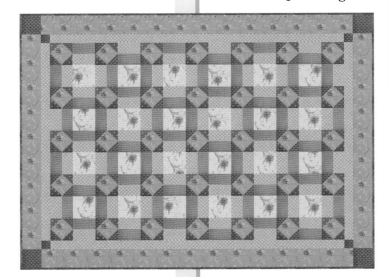

no shoes, no shirt, no service

button-down shirts

transformed

Before you give away any button-down shirts, consider salvaging the good parts of the oxford cloth to make the featured quilt. For "No Shoes, No Shirt, No Service," a collection of worn shirts was recycled to make the throw-sized quilt; in-tact sections of each shirt, such as the sleeves, front, and back, were used, as were the original shirt buttons that were snipped off the collars, cuffs, pockets, and shirt fronts.

*Note: Never use buttons or other small decorations on a quilt intended for babies or small children.

skill level
Easy

throw size
53" x 71" (1.35m x 1.80m)

finished block size
8" (20.32cm)

yardages
- 35 8½"(21.59cm) squares cut from assorted oxford cloth shirts
- ½ yd. (0.46m) white print fabric
- ⅞ yd. (0.80m) lt.-blue-print fabric
- ½ yd. (0.46m) lt.-green-print fabric
- 3⅜ yds. (3.09m) backing fabric, as desired
- 60"x 78"(1.52m x 1.98m) batting
- ⅜ yd. (0.34m) binding fabric, as desired

other materials
- 24 men's shirt buttons in assorted sizes*

Quilt made by Velda Grubbs, machine-quilted by Sherry Massey

cutting table — Based on a 42"-wide fabric

Fabric	Used for	FIRST CUT Number of pieces or crosswise strips	FIRST CUT Cut size	SECOND CUT Number of pieces or crosswise strips	SECOND CUT Cut size	THIRD CUT Number of pieces or crosswise strips	THIRD CUT Cut size
Various shirts	Blocks	35	8½" squares				
White print	Sashing	15	1½" strips	58	1½" x 8½" rectangles		
Light-blue print	Setting squares	1	1½" strip	24	1½" squares		
	Outer border	11	2" strips	Piece together and cut		4	2" x 44½" strips
						4	2" x 62½" strips
	Corner block squares	1	2" strip	16	2" squares		
Light-green print	Outer border	6	2" strips	Piece together and cut		2	2" x 44½" strips
						2	2" x 62½" strips
	Corner block squares	1	2" strip	20	2" squares		

Metric conversions for cutting table: 1½"(3.81cm)   2"(5.08cm)   8½"(21.59cm)   42"(1.07m)   44½"(1.13m)   62½"(1.59m)

NO SHIRT

QUILT ASSEMBLY

1. Sew five shirt squares and four 1½-in. x 8½-in. (3.81cm x 21.59cm) white rectangles together as shown in the diagram to make one five-block row.

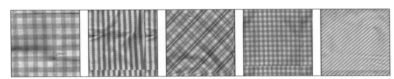

Repeat to make a total of seven five-block rows.

2. Sew five 1½-in. x 8½-in. (3.81cm x 21.59cm) white rectangles and four 1½ in.-(3.81cm) blue-print squares together as shown in the diagram to make one sashing row.

Repeat to make a total of six sashing rows.

3. Alternating block rows and sashing rows, sew the quilt center together. See the "Whole Quilt Diagram" on page 25.

Border Corner Blocks

1. Sew together five 2-in. (5.08cm) light-green-print squares and four 2-in. (5.08cm) light-blue print squares to make a "Border Corner Block," as shown.

Repeat to sew a total of four corner blocks.

1

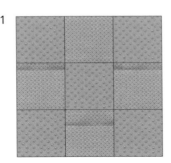

Outer Border

1. Sew together two 2-in. x 62 ½-in. (5.08cm x 1.59m) light-blue-print strips positioning one 2-in. x 62½-in. (5.08cm x 1.59m) light-green-print strip between the light-blue strips. See the "Whole Quilt Diagram" on page 25. Sew the three-strip border unit to one side of the quilt center. Iron. Repeat to make a border for the opposite side of the quilt.

2. Sew together two 2-in. x 44 ½-in. (5.08cm x 1.13m) light-blue print strips, positioning one 2-in. x 44½-in. (5.08cm x 1.13m) light-green-print strip in between the light-blue strips. See" Whole Quilt Diagram" on page 25. Sew one corner block to each end of the completed border strip. Sew the border to the top of the quilt. Repeat to make a border for the bottom of the quilt.

3. Optional: Use a threaded hand-sewing needle to sew a button to the center of each square.

FINISHING YOUR QUILT

1. Layer your quilt top, batting, and backing. See "Layering the Quilt," on page 118. Quilt as desired.

TIP

Save scraps of fabric, especially sturdy sections harvested from children's clothing long outgrown. The scraps can be made into a pieced quilt, forever reminding you of times gone by.

When you make the featured quilt in other fabrics, like flannel, consider using buttons in colors that match the colors of the flannel setting squares.

COLOR VARIATION

Another style approach is to use flannel shirts instead of oxford cloth shirts to make the quilted throw. Flannel comes in brown, rust, navy blue, and ochre, colors that are associated with folk art and that look great in more rustic interiors. Here, an assortment of flannel squares in plaids and stripes makes up the featured pattern. Accent the setting squares with antique buttons or ones made from embossed silver. Sew one to the center of each setting square, tying each with a heavy weight thread for added country style.

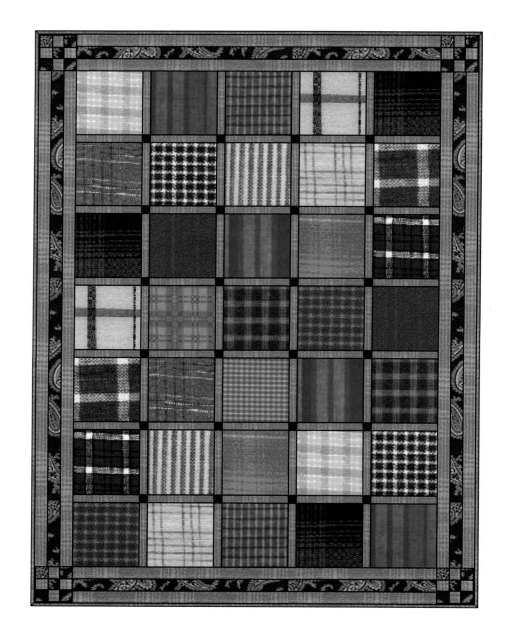

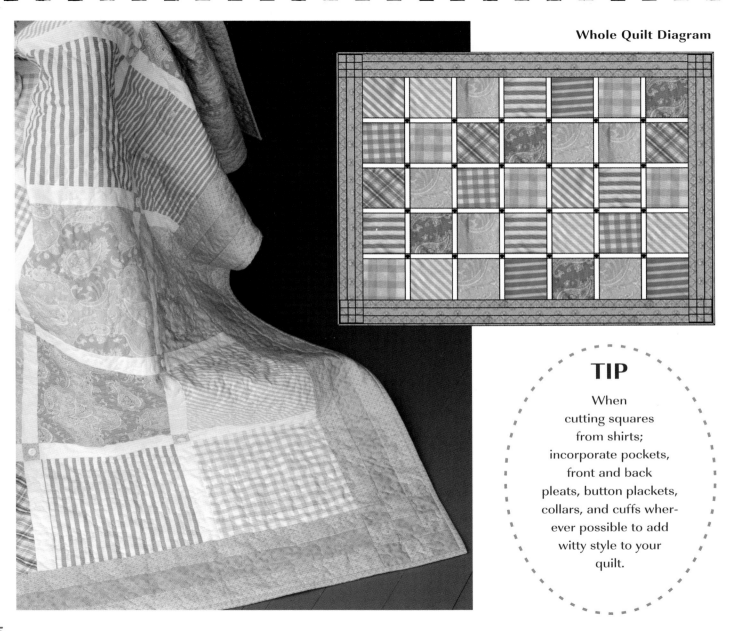

Whole Quilt Diagram

TIP

When cutting squares from shirts; incorporate pockets, front and back pleats, button plackets, collars, and cuffs wherever possible to add witty style to your quilt.

The charming appeal of this quilt is the juxtaposition of fresh pastel colors expressed in striped and plaid patterns.

block-down-drag-out

a feisty quilt with knockout color

The phrase "knock-down-drag-out" is usually reserved for a boxing match, but the only fight that might erupt over "Block-Down-Drag-Out" is who will be the recipient of the quilt. Vibrant with color and graphic punch, this quilt is a wonderful project for a beginner. A single patch, a four-patch, and a nine-patch are the only blocks used, making the quilt easy to construct. The quilt is made in brightly colored fabrics, or "brights," but it would be as attractive if made in pastels, or in soft, cuddly flannels. Consider this quilt design if the idea of sharing your quilting skills with an eager beginner appeals to you.

skill level
Easy

throw size
50" x 62" (1.27m x 1.57m)

block size
6" (15.24cm)

yardages
- ½ yd. (0.46m) total of various pink-print fabrics
- ½ yd. (0.46m) total of various blue-print fabrics
- ½ yd. (0.46m) total of various green-print fabrics
- ½ yd. (0.46m) total of various yellow-print fabrics
- ½ yd. (0.46m) blue-print fabric
- 1 yd. (0.91m) plaid fabric
- 3¼ yds. (2.97m) backing, as desired
- 56" x 68" (1.42m x 1.73m) batting
- ⅜ yd. (0.34m) binding, as desired

Quilt made by Sharon Olson, machine-quilted by Sherry Massey

cutting table Based on a 42"-wide fabric

Fabric	Used for	FIRST CUT Number of pieces or crosswise strips	Cut size	SECOND CUT Number of pieces or crosswise strips	Cut size	THIRD CUT Number of pieces or crosswise strips	Cut size
Various pink, blue, green, purple and yellow prints	Nine-patch blocks	108	1½" squares				
	Four-patch blocks	20	2½" squares				
	Solid blocks	31	3½" squares				
Blue print	Inner border	5	2½" strips	Piece together and cut		2	2½" x 48½"
						2	
Plaid	Outer border	6	5½" strips	Piece together and cut		2	5½" x 52½"
						2	5½" x 50½"

Metric conversions for cutting table: 1½"(3.81cm) 2½"(6.35cm) 3½"(8.89cm) 5½"(13.97cm) 42"(1.07m) 48½"(1.23m) 50½"(1.28m) 52½"(1.33m)

BLOCK-DOWN-DRAG-OUT

BLOCK ASSEMBLY

Nine-Patch Block

1. Sew together three 2½-in. (6.35cm) squares in various prints, as shown.

2. Repeat step 1 two more times to make a total of three strip sets. Iron two of the strip sets toward the middle. Iron one strip set outward. Sew the three strip sets together as shown in the diagram.

3. Repeat steps 1–2 11 more times to make a total of 12 nine-patch blocks.

1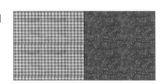

2

Four-Patch Block

1. Sew together two 3½-in. (8.89cm) squares in various prints, as shown. Iron. Repeat. Iron.

2. Sew the two strip sets together as shown in the diagram. Iron.

3. Repeat steps 1–2 four more times, for a total of five four-patch blocks.

QUILT ASSEMBLY

1. Referring to the "Whole Quilt Diagram," on page 31, sew together six blocks across and eight blocks down to make the quilt center, mixing in the nine-patch blocks, the four-patch blocks, and the 6½-in. (16.51cm) squares of various prints. Iron.

Inner Border

1. Sew a 2½-in. x 48½-in. (6.35cm x 1.23m) blue print strip on each side of the quilt center. Iron.

2. Sew a 2½-in. x 40½-in. (6.35cm x 1.03m) blue print strip to the top and the bottom of the quilt center. Iron.

Outer Border

1. Sew a 5½-in. x 52½-in. (13.97cm x 1.33m) plaid strip to each side of the quilt center. Iron.

2. Sew a 5½-in. x 50½-in. (13.97cm x 1.28m) plaid strip to the top of the quilt center. Repeat to sew a strip to the bottom of the quilt center. Iron.

FINISHING YOUR QUILT

1. Layer your quilt top, batting, and backing. See "Layering the Quilt," on page 118. Quilt as desired.

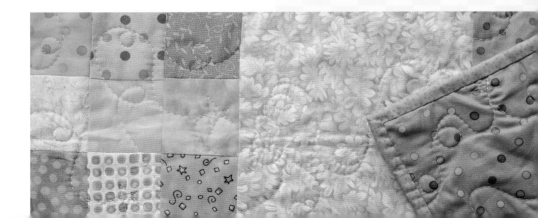

The vast array of colors and patterns in jewel tones in this quilt make it a stylish addition to any room. The quilt can go from bold and flirty to alluring and chic depending on the color and pattern of your home furnishings.

COLOR VARIATION

Bright quilt colors always look amazing, but a more quiet palette can also create stylistic impact when the block design is bold as is featured here. This quilt is so surprisingly fast and easy to make that you may be inspired to make another in the same pattern using fabrics in autumnal colors.

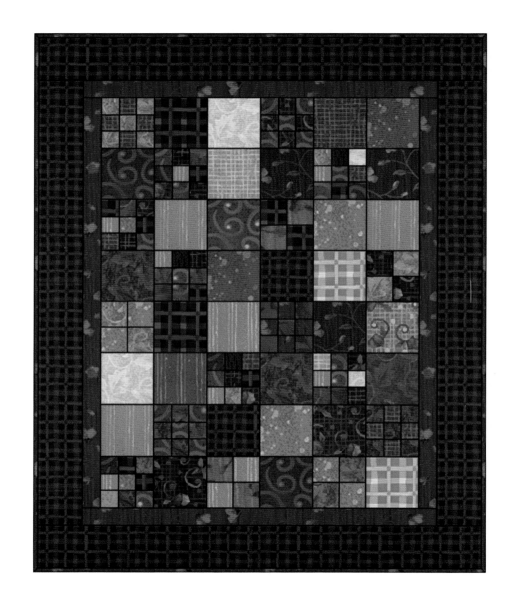

Whole Quilt Diagram

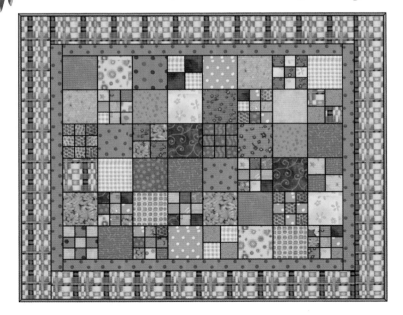

hanky panky

flirtation with the past

Vintage decorative hankies (or handkerchiefs, as they are formally called) are a surprising source of fabric for romantically-styled quilts. The small squares of cotton are screen-printed with delicate florals and dainty patterns in soft colors, each unique design an appealing part of this quick and easy quilt made in wall-hanging size. Each hankie is cut into fours, backed, and bordered, or "sashed," to make up each quilt block. Whether you use treasured family heirlooms, fabulous flea market finds, or new reproductions, "Hanky Panky" can be easily made in a weekend.

Note: To avoid fading, never display quilts in direct sunlight.

skill level
Easy

wallhanging
55" x 55" (1.40m x 1.40m)

block size
12½" (31.75cm)

yardages
- 1¾ yds. (1.60m) solid white fabric
- 1⅛ yds. (1.03m) green print
- ⅜ yd. (0.34m) pink print
- 3½ yds. (3.20m) backing fabric, as desired
- 60" x 60" batting (1.52m x 1.52m)
- ⅜ yd. (0.34m) binding fabric, as desired

other materials
- 16 screen-printed hankies, 11.5"–12" (29.21cm–30.48cm) square, laundered, and ironed

Quilt made by Velda Grubbs, machine-quilted by Sherry Massey

cutting table Based on a 42"-wide fabric

| Fabric | Used for | FIRST CUT | | SECOND CUT | | THIRD CUT | |
		Number of pieces or crosswise strips	Cut size	Number of pieces or crosswise strips	Cut size	Number of pieces or crosswise strips	Cut size
16 hankies	Blocks	Cut each hanky in quarters to make four 5¾" squares (64 total). Keep squares from same hanky together.					
White solid	Hanky lining	10	5¾" strips	64	5¾" squares		
Green print	Sashing	16	1½" strips	112	1½" x 5½" rectangles		
	Outer border	6	2" strips	Piece together and cut		2	2½" x 51½" strips
						2	2½" x 54½" strips
Pink print	Setting squares	2	1½" strips	49	1½" squares		
	Inner border	5	1½" strips	Piece together and cut		2	1½" x 49½" strips
						2	1½" x 51½" strips

Metric conversions for cutting table: 1½"(3.81cm) 2"(5.08cm) 2½"(6.35cm) 5½"(13.97cm) 5¾"(14.61cm) 42"(1.07m) 49½"(1.26m) 51½"(1.31m) 54½"(1.38m)

HANKY PANKY

BLOCK CONSTRUCTION

1. Using four 5¾-in. (14.61cm) squares cut from the same hanky and four 5¾-in. (14.61cm) squares of white hanky lining, back each hanky square, right side facing up, with one white square. Iron the layers together, handling them as one. Sew one 1½-in. x 5¾-in. (3.81cm x 14.61cm) green-print strip between two squares, ironing all the seams toward the green print, and making sure the center motif of the hanky is positioned at or near the center of the unit. Repeat.

2. To make sashing unit, sew together two 1½-in. x 5¾-in. (3.81cm x 14.61cm) green-print rectangles and one 1½-in. (3.81cm) pink-print square in a row.

3. Sew together two hanky units prepared in step 1 and one sashing unit made in step 2. Repeat using the remaining 15 hankies to make a total of 16 large blocks.

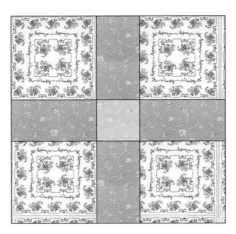

QUILT ASSEMBLY

1. Sew together two 1½-in. x 5¾-in. (3.81cm x 14.61cm) green-print rectangles and one 1½-in. (3.81cm) pink-print square (sashing unit) to make a sashing strip, referring to the diagram in step 2 of "Block Construction," if needed. Repeat to make a total of 24 sashing strips.

2. Sew together four large blocks and three sashing strips to complete a row of blocks. Repeat three times to make a total of four rows of blocks.

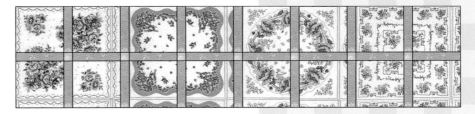

3. Sew together four sashing strips and three 1½-in. (3.81cm) pink-print squares to make a sashing row. Repeat two times to make a total of three sashing rows.

4. Alternating block rows and sashing rows, sew the quilt center together, referring to the "Whole Quilt Diagram" on page 37.

ADDING BORDERS
Inner Framing Border

1. Sew a 1½-in. x 49½-in. (3.81cm x 1.26m) strip of pink print to each side of the quilt center. Iron.

2. Sew a 1½-in. x 51½-in. (3.81cm x 1.31m) strip of pink print to the top of the quilt center and one to the bottom. Iron.

COLOR VARIATION

What an exquisite little quilt! Made as directed in "Hanky Panky," this variation uses floral and fruit fabrics instead of vintage-style hankies to make up the sashed blocks. The juxtaposition of the fabric prints appears random, but the medium robin's egg blue and strawberry colorway (with surprising blocks in pale yellow) tie the design neatly together. Small in size, the wall hanging can accent the arm of a couch in a solid, coordinating color, providing dynamic pattern and style.

Color plays a prominent role in conveying style. When a colorway changes from pale pastels to rich gem tones, the style vibe shifts from subtle, sweet, and fresh to bold and traditional.

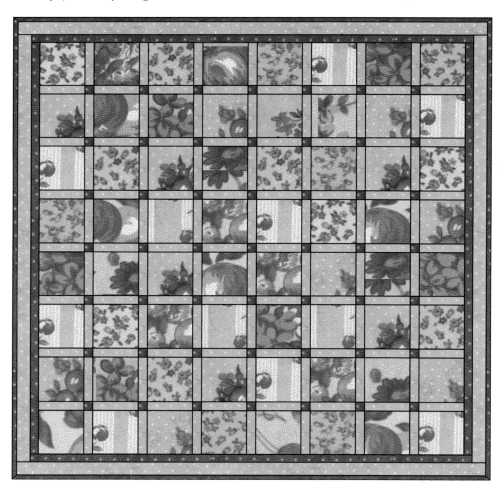

Outer Border

1. Sew a 2-in. x 51½-in. (5.08cm x 1.31m) strip of green print to each side of the quilt center. Iron.

2. Sew one 2-in. x 54½-in. (5.08cm x 1.38m) strip of green print to the top of the quilt center and one to the bottom. Iron.

FINISHING YOUR QUILT

1. Layer the quilt top, batting, and backing. See "Layering the Quilt," on page 118. Quilt as desired.

Whole Quilt Diagram

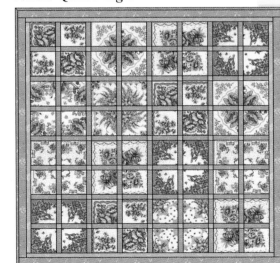

TIP

Choose hankies that have an outer border or a corner motif. Fold each hanky in quarters to get an idea how it will look in a four-patch block. When recycling vintage hankies, wash them first, then iron them before cutting.

purple pickle lily

country fair and lovely

The inspiration for this design was drawn from two sweet and simple pleasures found at a country fair, pickles and lilies. Drawing inspiration from their distinct colors (brightened up a bit), "Purple Pickle Lily" is a quick and uncomplicated quilt that uses a classic "log-cabin block" set on point for its construction. The log-cabin quilt pattern is one in which two dark strips and two light-fabric strips are sewn on adjacent sides around a center square. Although the quilt pattern is very old, there is nothing old-fashioned about the vibrant colorway of this wall-hanging-size quilt done in the same pattern.

skill level
Intermediate

wall hanging size
51¼" x 51¼"(1.30m x 1.30m)

block size
8"(20.32cm)

yardages
- ¼ yd. (0.23m) pink print fabric #1
- ⅜ yd. (0.34m) pink print fabric #2
- ½ yd. (0.46m) pink print fabric #3
- ⅜ yd. (0.34m) purple print fabric #1
- ⅜ yd. (0.34m) purple print fabric #2
- 1½ yds. (1.37m) purple print fabric #3
- ⅜ yd. (0.34m) green print fabric
- 3¼ yds. (2.97m) backing, as desired
- 57" x 57" batting (1.45m x 1.45m)
- ⅜ yd. (0.34m) binding fabric, as desired

Quilt made by Dianna Olson, machine-quilted by Sherry Massey

cutting table — Based on a 42"-wide fabric

Fabric	Used for	FIRST CUT		SECOND CUT		THIRD CUT	
		Number of pieces or crosswise strips	Cut size	Number of pieces or crosswise strips	Cut size	Number of pieces or crosswise strips	Cut size
Pink print #1 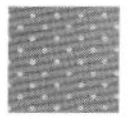	Blocks	4	1½" strips				
Pink print #2 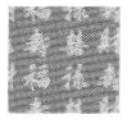	Blocks	7	1½" strips				
Pink print #3 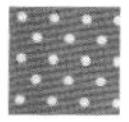	Blocks	10	1½" strips				
Purple print #1 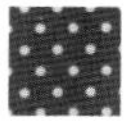	Blocks	6	1½" strips				
Purple print #2 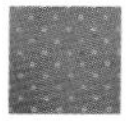	Blocks	8	1½" strips				
Purple print #3 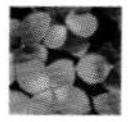	Blocks	10	1½" strips				
	Corner triangles	1	6⅝" strip	2	6⅝" squares	Cut once diagonally	
	Side triangles	1	12⅝" strip	3	12⅝" squares	Cut twice diagonally	
	Border	5	2½" strips	Piece together and cut		4	2½" x 47¾"
Green print	Blocks	2	2½" strips	29	2½" squares		
	border	5	1½" strips	Piece together and cut		2	2½" x 47¾"
						2	2½" x 47¾"

Metric conversions for cutting table: 1½"(3.81cm) 2½"(6.35cm) 6⅝"(16.83cm) 12⅝"(32.07cm) 42"(1.07m) 47¾"(1.21m)

PURPLE PICKLE LILY

QUILT ASSEMBLY

Block

1. Sew a 1½-in. (3.81cm) pink-print #1 strip to the edge of a 2½-in. (6.35cm) green-print square. Trim the edge of the 2½-in. (6.35cm) square. Iron.

2. Sew a 1½-in. (3.81cm) pink-print #1 strip to the edge of the unit. Trim the edge. Iron.

3. Continue to add two 1½-in. (3.81cm) purple-print #1 strips. Trim and iron after each addition.

4. Continue sewing 1½-in. (3.81cm) strips to the block, with two sections of each color in the following order: pink-print #2, purple-print #2, pink-print #3, and purple-print #3. Trim and iron after each addition.

1

2

3

4

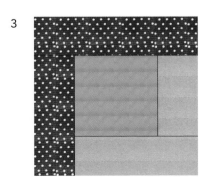

5. Repeat steps 1–4 24 times to make a total of 25 blocks.

QUILT ASSEMBLY

1. Sew the adjacent rows together. See "Construction Diagram" on page 43.

Inner Border

1. Sew a 1½-in. x 45¾-in. (3.81cm x 1.16m) green-print strip to each side of the quilt center. Iron.

2. Sew one 1½-in. x 47¾-in. (3.81cm x 1.21m) green-print strip to the top and the bottom of the quilt center.

Outer Border

1. Sew a 2½-in. x 47¾-in. (6.35cm x 1.21m) purple-print #3 strip to each side of the quilt. Iron.

2. Sew one 2½-in. (6.35cm) green-print square to each end of two 2½-in. x 47¾-in. (6.35cm x 1.21m) purple-print #3 strips. Sew the strip to the top edge of the quilt center. Repeat for the bottom.

FINISHING YOUR QUILT

1. Layer your quilt top, batting and backing. Quilt as desired.

TIP

The bold contrasts in color in the log-cabin block are created by sewing strips of dark fabric on two adjacent sides of the central square and sewing strips of lighter fabric on the other two sides. Once you are familiar with this quilt pattern, you may not need to measure. Instead, cut a bunch of equally-wide strips in light and dark fabrics, and sew them and cut them as you work. Cut off each strip to the needed length as you sew.

COLOR VARIATION

I t is amazing to see how different a log-cabin quilt pattern can look when the fabrics are changed from one set of colors to another. Here, the pattern accentuates the brown fabrics, which appear to move foward while the green fabrics recede. The optical illusion can work in an interior design, accentuating the prominent brown color, such as polished woods and fabrics in richer earth tones.

The versatile log-cabin pattern can be worked so that the dark and light fabrics are used on opposite sides of the central square.

Log-Cabin Shortcut

When sewing a strip of fabric that is longer than needed to the block, trim off the excess fabric as follows: iron the seam, and lay the block on a cutting mat so that the excess strip extends to the right. Align the top edge of a ruler with the top edge of the strip, with the end of the ruler even and perpendicular to the side of the block. Use a rotary cutter or scissors to trim the excess strip even with the edge of the ruler. Do this after adding each strip to keep the block square.

Construction Diagram

rosy outlook

a fresh, floral feel

Make a beautiful bed of "roses" in your bedroom using this quilt and matching pillowcases to set the scene. The overall design of "Rosy Outlook" is centered around one of nature's most elegant and unparalleled gifts; the rose. Pastel fabrics with floral motifs and rose prints make up the quilt. While old-fashioned in sensibility, they confer an aire of Victorian elegance. Although "Rosy Outlook" is more time-consuming than other quilts in "The Collection," its ease of assembly and the shear beauty of the design will more than make up for your effort. Along the way, it will inspire a rosy outlook.

skill level
Intermediate

queen size
88" x 97" (2.24m x 2.46m)

block size
9" (22.86cm)

yardages
- 2⅛ yds. (1.94m) pink-floral print
- ⅝ yd. (0.57m) purple-floral print
- ⅞ yd. (0.80m) green-floral print
- ⅜ yd. (0.34m) med.-pink print
- ¾ yd. (0.69m) various light-pink prints
- ⅜ yd. (0.34m) med.-purple prints
- ¾ yd. (0.69m) various lt.-purple prints
- ¾ yd. (0.69m) med.-green print
- ¾ yd. (0.69m) various lt.-green prints
- ⅜ yd. (0.34m) med.-blue print
- ¾ yd. (0.69m) various lt.-blue prints
- ⅝ yd. (0.57m) lt.-purple-dot print
- 7⅞ yds. (7.20m) backing fabric, as desired
- 94" x 103" (2.39m x 2.62m) batting
- ⅝ yd.(0.57m) binding fabric, as desired

Quilt made by Velda Grubbs, machine-quilted by Sherry Massey.

cutting table

Based on a 42"-wide fabric

Fabric	Used for	FIRST CUT		SECOND CUT		THIRD CUT	
		Number of pieces or crosswise strips	Cut size	Number of pieces or crosswise strips	Cut size	Number of pieces or crosswise strips	Cut size
Pink floral	Blocks	2	9½" strips	3	9½" squares		
	Border	10	5½" strips	Piece together and cut		2	5½" x 87½"
						2	5½" x 88½"
Purple floral	Blocks	2	9½" strips	10	9½" squares		
Green floral	Blocks	3	9½" strips	10	9½" squares		
Blue floral	Blocks	3	9½" strips	8	9½" squares		
Medium-pink print	Blocks	6	2" strips				
Various light-pink prints	Blocks	12	2" strips				
Medium-purple print	Blocks	6	2" strips				

cutting table (continued)

Fabric	Used for	FIRST CUT		SECOND CUT		THIRD CUT	
		Number of pieces or crosswise strips	Cut size	Number of pieces or crosswise strips	Cut size	Number of pieces or crosswise strips	Cut size
Various light-purple prints	Blocks	12	2" strips				
Medium-green print	Blocks	6	2" strips				
	Middle border	9	1½" strips	Piece together and cut		2	1½" x 78½"
						2	1½" x 85½"
Various light-green prints	Blocks	12	2" strips				
Medium-blue print	Blocks	6	2" strips				
Various light-blue prints	Blocks	12	2" strips				
Purple print	Border	8	2½" strips	Piece together and cut		2	1½" x 78½"
						2	1½" x 78½"

Metric conversions for cutting table: 1½"(3.81cm) 2"(5.08cm) 2½"(6.35cm) 5½"(13.97cm) 9½"(24.13cm) 42"(1.07m) 78½"(2.00m) 85½"(2.17m) 87½"(2.22m) 88½"(2.25m)

Rosy Outlook Template

After completing a project that uses a template, store the template in a large envelope. Tape the envelope to the inside cover of your pattern book so that it is ready to use when you need it again. Be sure to write the project name on the template for quick reference. See "Making a Template," on page 114, for instructions.

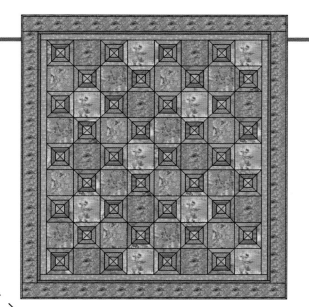

Whole Quilt Diagram

Rosy Outlook Template

Quilting is a personal pursuit that allows you to enter a world of imagination filled with color and pattern.

ROSY OUTLOOK

BLOCK CONSTRUCTION

1. Sew one 2-in.-wide (5.08cm) medium-pink-print strip and two 2-in.-wide (5.08cm) various pink-print strips together lengthwise, with the medium-pink-print strip in the middle. Iron the seams toward middle strip. Repeat five times for a total of six pink strip sets.

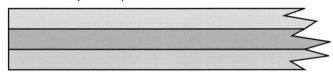

2. Repeat step 1 to make six purple strip sets, ironing the seams toward the outer strip, six green strip sets, ironing the seams toward the middle strip, and six blue strip sets, ironing the seams toward the outer strips.

3. Using the template on page 48, cut six triangles from each strip set, making a total of 36 triangles, or six from each color combination. See "Making a Template," on page 114, for directions on making a triangle template.

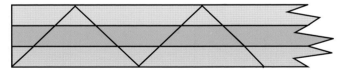

4. To assemble blocks: sew together four triangle strip sets in color combinations to make 20 Block As and 16 Block Bs.

A 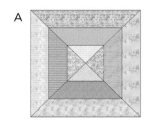 B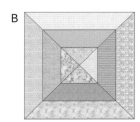

Note: Blues and purples are reversed in Block A and Block B.

QUILT ASSEMBLY

1. Following the "Whole Quilt Diagram" on page 48, sew the blocks together to make a quilt top with nine rows of eight blocks, alternating the pieced blocks and the 9½-in. (24.13cm) square floral blocks.
Note: Use Block As in the odd-numbered rows (1, 3, 5 etc.) and Block Bs in the even-numbered rows (2, 4, 6 etc.). Iron.

ADDING BORDERS

Inner Border:

1. Sew a 2½-in. x 81½-in. (6.35cm x 2.07m) purple strip to each side of the quilt center. Iron.

2. Sew a 2½-in. x 76½-in. (6.35cm x 1.94m) purple strip to the top and bottom of the quilt center.

Middle Border

1. Sew a 1½-in. x 85½-in. (3.81cm x 2.17m) medium-green strip to each side of the quilt. Iron.

2. Sew a 1½-in. x 78½-in. (3.81cm x 2.00m) medium-green strip to the top and bottom of the quilt. Iron.

Outer Border

1. Sew a 5½-in. x 87½-in. (13.97cm x 2.22m) pink-floral strip to each side of the quilt. Iron.

2. Sew a 5½-in. x 88½-in. (13.97cm x 2.25m) pink-floral strip to the top and bottom of the quilt. Iron.

FINISHING YOUR QUILT

1. Layer your quilt top, batting, and backing. See "Layering the Quilt," on page 118. Quilt as desired.

cutting table   Based on 42"-wide fabric

Fabric for pillowcases	Used for	FIRST CUT		SECOND CUT		THIRD CUT	
		Number of pieces or crosswise strips	Cut size	Number of pieces or crosswise strips	Cut size	Number of pieces or crosswise strips	Cut size
Main fabric	Case	2	25" strips	2	25" x 41" rectangles		
Floral fabric	Band	2	12½" strips	2	12½" x 41" rectangles		
Accent fabric	Trim	2	3" strips	2	3" x 41" strips		

Metric conversions for cutting table: 3"(7.62cm) 12½"(31.75cm) 25"(63.50cm) 41"(1.04m) 42"(1.07m)

TIP

Create a coordinated look in any bedroom by making matching pillowcases for any of the quilts in "The Collection." Simply follow the directions on page 51.

COLOR VARIATION

This color option is fabulous, combining various colors that compliment each other nicely. The bright green in the pillow case effectively offsets the deeper colors incorporated into the quilt.

MATCHING PILLOWCASES

Note: Use ½-in. (1.27cm) seams throughout the project.

1. Fold one 25-in. x 41-in. (63.50cm x 1.04m) rectangle of the main fabric in half, right sides together. It will measure 20½ in. x 24½ in. (52.07cm x 62.23cm) after folding. Sew across one end and down one side. Trim off the corner where the seams cross as shown. Turn the case right side out. Iron.

2. Fold one 12½-in. x 41-in. (31.75cm x 1.04m) floral-fabric rectangle in half, right sides together. Sew across the short ends to create a tube. Iron the seam open. Fold the tube in half, wrong sides together. Iron. Slip the tube inside the case, and pin along the raw edge, matching side seams.

3. Fold one 3-in. x 41-in. (7.62cm x 1.04m) accent-fabric strip, right sides together, and stitch across the short ends to create a tube. Iron the seam open. Slip the tube inside the case, right side facing the floral fabric, and pin along the raw edge, matching the side seams. Stitch the layers together using a ½-in. (1.27cm) seam.

4. Fold and iron the accent trim in half, raw edges even. Fold under a ½-in. (1.27cm) hem along the raw edge. Iron the trim toward the lower edge of the case. Pin the hem on the trim to the case along the fold, trapping all raw edges in between. Top stitch through all layers a scant ⅛ in. (31.75cm) from the seam line. Repeat for the second pillowcase.

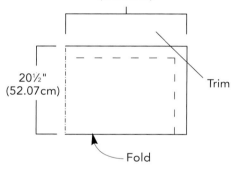

25"
(63.50cm)

20½"
(52.07cm)

Trim

Fold

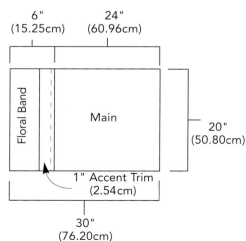

6"
(15.25cm)

24"
(60.96cm)

Floral Band

Main

20"
(50.80cm)

1" Accent Trim
(2.54cm)

30"
(76.20cm)

skill level

Easy

size

20" x 20" (50.80cm x 50.80cm)
(two cases)

yardages

■ 1½ yds. (1.37m) main fabric

■ ¾ yd. (0.69m) floral fabric

■ ¼ yd. (0.23m) accent fabric

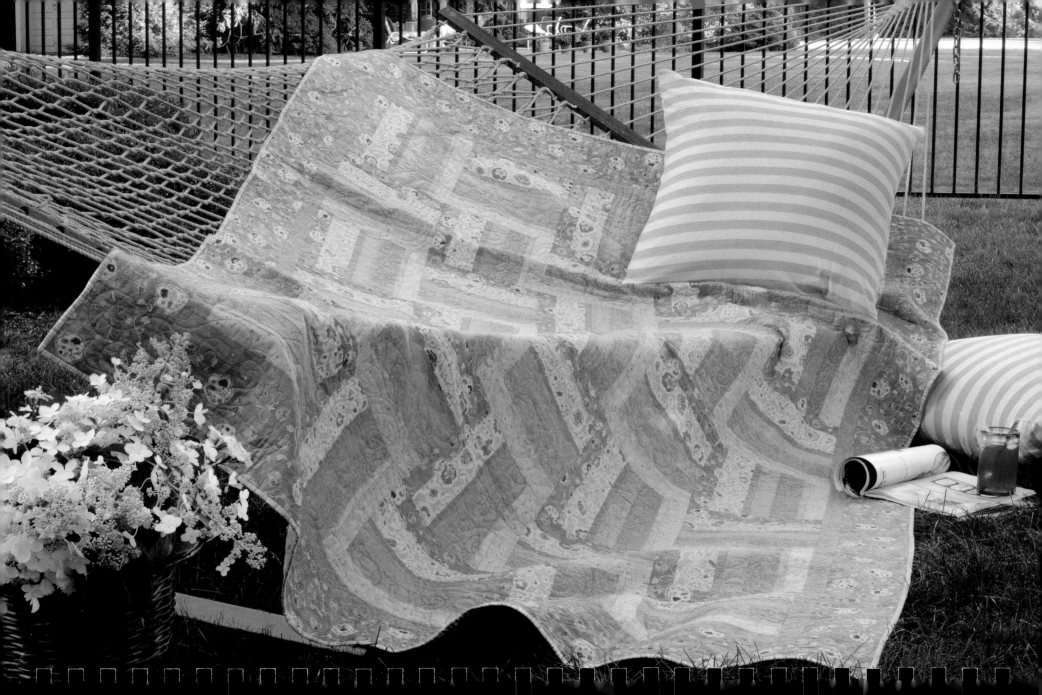

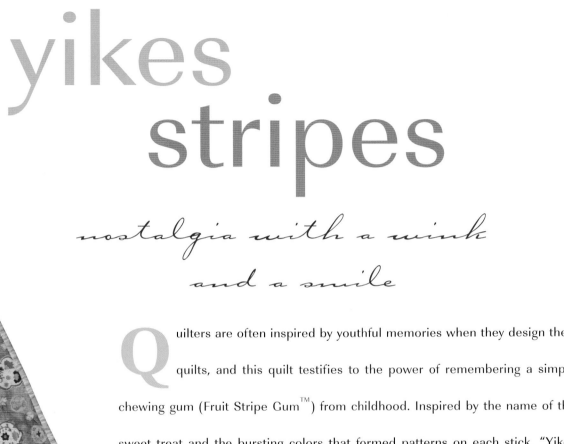

yikes stripes

nostalgia with a wink and a smile

Quilters are often inspired by youthful memories when they design their quilts, and this quilt testifies to the power of remembering a simple chewing gum (Fruit Stripe Gum™) from childhood. Inspired by the name of the sweet treat and the bursting colors that formed patterns on each stick, "Yikes Stripes" uses fabric stripes in deliciously fruity colors in blocks constructed in a playful mix of pink, green, and blue stripes and a stripe in buttercup yellow added for extra fun. Making each quilt block is easy, as is putting the blocks together to make the whole quilt.

skill level
Easy

twin size
63" x 93" (1.60m x 2.36m)

block size
10" (25.40cm)

yardages
- ■ 2⅛ yds. (1.94m) pink print
- ■ 1¼ yds. (1.14m) green print
- ■ ⅞ yd. (0.80m) blue-dot print
- ■ ⅞ yd. (0.80m) yellow-tonal print
- ■ 1⅛ yds. (1.03m) blue-tonal print
- ■ ½ yd. (0.46m) green-marble print
- ■ ⅞ yd. (0.80m) pink-dot print
- ■ 5⅞ yds. (5.37m) backing fabric, as desired
- ■ 70" x 100" (1.78m x 2.54m) batting
- ■ ½ yd. (0.46m) binding fabric, as desired

Quilted by Velda Grubbs, machine-quilted by Sherry Massey

cutting table Based on 42"-wide fabric

Fabric	Used for	FIRST CUT		SECOND CUT		THIRD CUT	
		Number of pieces or crosswise strips	Cut size	Number of pieces or crosswise strips	Cut size	Number of pieces or crosswise strips	Cut size
Pink print	Blocks	14	2" strips			2	5½" x 83½"
	Outer border	8	5½" strips			2	5½" x 63½"
Green print	Blocks	14	3" strips				
Blue-dot print	Blocks	14	1" strips			2	2" x 80½"
	Inner border	7	2" strips	Piece together and cut		2	2" x 53½"
Yellow-tonal print	Blocks	14	2" strips				
Blue-tonal print	Blocks	14	2½" strips				
Green-marble print	Blocks	14	1" strips				
Pink-dot print	Blocks	14	2" strips				

Metric conversions for cutting table: 1"(2.54cm)   2"(5.08cm)   2½"(6.35cm)   3"(7.62cm)   5½"(13.97cm)   42"(1.07m)   53½"(1.36m)   63½"(1.61m)   80½"(2.04m)
83½"(2.12m)

YIKES STRIPES

BLOCK CONSTRUCTION

1. Sew a 2-in.-wide (5.08cm) pink-print strip and a 3-in.-wide (7.62cm) green-print strip together. Add a 1-in.-wide (2.54cm) blue-dot strip next to the green-print strip. Continue adding strips in this order: 2-in.-wide (5.08cm) yellow-tonal print, 2½-in.-wide (6.35cm) blue-tonal print, 1-in.-wide (2.54cm) green-marble print, and 2-in.-wide (5.08cm) pink-dot. Iron.
Note: refer to the diagram in step 2, as needed.

2. Cut the construction made in step 1 into three 10½-in.-wide (26.67cm) blocks. Repeat to make 40 blocks.

QUILT ASSEMBLY

1. Referring to the "Whole Quilt Diagram" on page 57 for block placement, sew the blocks together in 8 rows of 5 blocks each. Iron.

ADDING BORDERS

Inner Border

1. Sew one 2-in. x 80½-in. (5.08cm x 2.04m) blue-dot strip to the sides of the quilt center. Iron.

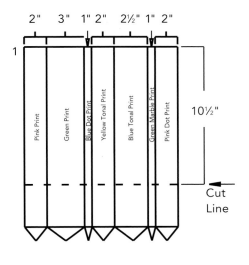

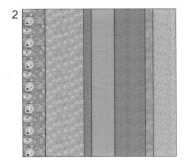

2. Sew one 2-in. x 53½-in. (5.08cm x 1.36m) blue-dot strip to the top and bottom of the quilt center. Iron.

Outer Border

1. Sew one 5½-in. x 83½-in. (13.97cm x 2.12m) pink-print strip to each side of the quilt. Iron.

2. Sew one 5½-in. x 63½-in. (13.97cm x 1.61m) pink-print strip to the top and the bottom of the quilt. Iron.

FINISHING THE QUILT

Layer the quilt top, batting, and backing. See "Layering the Quilt," on page 118. Quilt as desired.

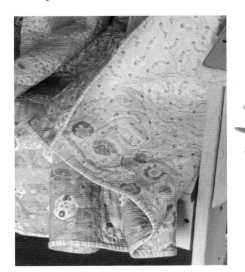

TIP

When sewing multiple strips together to form a "strip set," shorten the stitch length used on the sewing machine to prevent the stitch lines from pulling apart when the strips are cut into smaller sections.

Creating your own patchwork block designs is fun and rewarding, especially with a basic design that uses strips of fabric. Coordinate the colors of the stripes in the blocks with those in your soft furnishings.

COLOR VARIATION

A quilt using the conservative colors and patterns shown in this variation would also appeal to anyone who prefers more subdued colors than those used in the featured "Yikes..." original. To help children who share a room reveal their own sense of style, ask each to name his favorite color, and create companion quilts in coordinating colors.

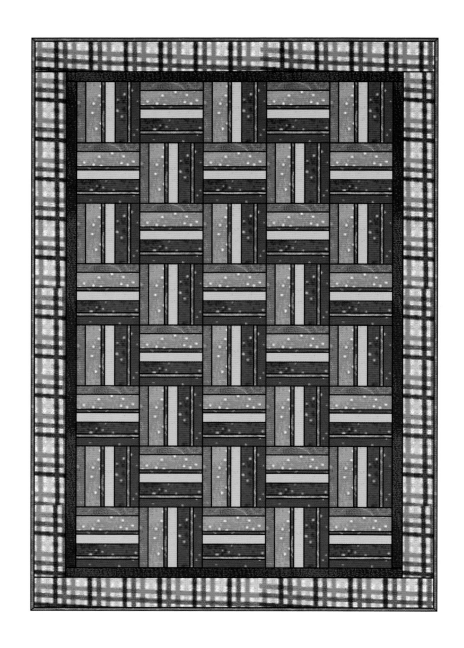

Whole Quilt Diagram

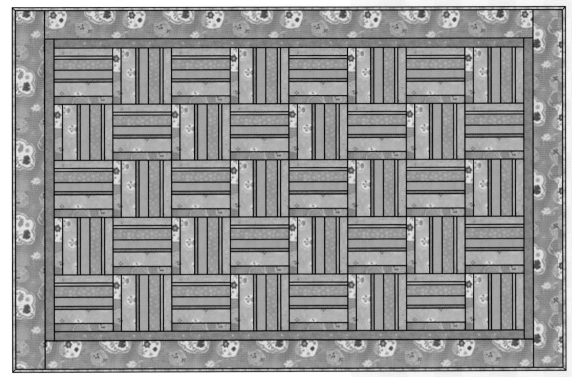

Little compares with the peaceful luxury of relaxing outdoors wrapped in a quilt pieced by a loved one.

giddy
walk

a souvenir of a milestone

What better way to remember an important milestone in your family's life than by making a quilt? Here, the first steps of a young child named Gideon* inspired this bright little quilt, made to fit a toddler-sized bed. The brilliantly-colored squares are arranged in the center of each block, forming an "X," a coincidental reference to the many cross-roads to which he may come in life. The beauty of any quilt is that it can be displayed in a room long after it has served its original and practical purpose.

*Gideon Michael Massey is the grandson of Sherry Massey, the quilter who machine-quilted all of the quilts in "The Collection."

skill level
Easy/Intermediate

toddler size
44" x 54" (1.12m x 1.37m)

block size
10" (25.40cm)

yardages
- ⅛ yd. (0.11m) each of 20 various bright prints
- ⅝ yd. (0.57m) green print
- ⅜ yd. (0.34m) dark-blue print
- ⅝ yd. (0.57m) medium-blue print
- ⅝ yd. (0.57m) white print
- 2⅞ yds. (2.63m) backing fabric, as desired
- 50" x 60" (1.27m x 1.52m) batting
- ⅜ yd. (0.34m) binding fabric, as desired

Quilt made by Dianna Olson, machine-quilted by Sherry Massey

cutting table   Based on a 42"-wide fabric

Fabric	Used for	FIRST CUT		SECOND CUT		THIRD CUT	
		Number of pieces or crosswise strips	Cut size	Number of pieces or crosswise strips	Cut size	Number of pieces or crosswise strips	Cut size
Various bright prints 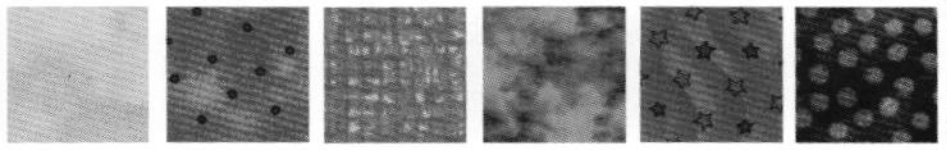	Blocks	1	2¼" strip from each fabric	20	5⅞" squares		1½" x 44½"
Green print 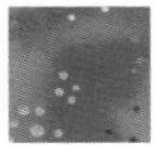	Border	7	2½" strips	16	2½" x 6½"		
				16	2½" x 9"		
				4	2½" squares		
Dark-blue print 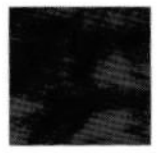	Border blocks	2	2½" strips	32	2½" squares		
	Corner blocks	1	3½" strip	4	3½" squares		
				4	2½" squares		
Medium-blue print 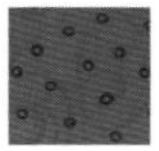	Border	5	3½" strips	Piece together and cut		2	3½" x 38½"
						2	3½" x 48½"
White print	Blocks	2	3⅛" strips	24	3⅜" squares	Cut in half once diagonally	
		2	6¼" strips	12	6¼" squares	Cut in half once diagonally	

Metric conversions for cutting table: 1½"(3.81m)   2¼"(5.72cm)   2½"(6.35cm)   3⅛"(7.94cm)   3⅜"(8.57cm)   3½"(8.89cm)   5⅞"(14.92cm)   6¼"(15.88cm)
6½"(16.51cm)   9"(22.86cm)   38½"(97.79cm)   42"(1.07m)   42½"(1.08m)   44½"(1.13m)   48½"(1.23m)

GIDDY WALK

QUILT ASSEMBLY

Blocks

1. Sew any two 2¼-in.-wide (5.72cm) bright-print strips together lengthwise. Iron.

2. From the strip set made in step 1, cut 12 2¼-in.-wide (5.72cm) strip-set segments.

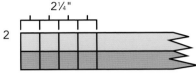

2¼"

3. Repeat with the 18 remaining 2¼-in.-wide (5.72cm) strips to make a total of ten strip sets. From each strip set, cut 12 2¼-in.-wide (5.72cm) strip-set segments.

4. Sew two strip-set segments together to make a four-patch unit. Iron. Repeat with the remaining strip-set segments to make a total of 60 four-patch units.

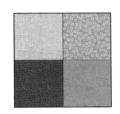

5. Make two As by sewing a four-patch unit, a 3⅜-in. (8.57cm) white-print triangle, and two 6¼-in. (15.88cm) white-print triangles together. Repeat.

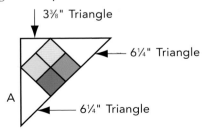

3⅜" Triangle

6¼" Triangle

6¼" Triangle

A

B

3⅜" Triangle

3⅜" Triangle

6. Make one B by sewing three four-patch units and two 3⅜-in. (8.57cm) white-print triangles together as shown. Iron.

7. Refer to the "Construction Diagram" to sew the block together. Iron.

8. Repeat steps 4–7 to make a total of 12 blocks.

9. Sew three blocks across and four blocks down to make the quilt center. See the "Whole Quilt Diagram" on page 63. Iron.

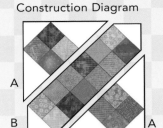

Construction Diagram

A

B

A

Inner Border

1. Sew four 2½-in. x 9-in. (6.35cm x 22.86cm) green-print rectangles and three 2½-in. (6.35cm) dark-blue-print squares together as shown. Iron. Sew the border to one side of the quilt center. Repeat for the other side. Iron.

2. Sew four 2½-in. x 6½-in. (6.35cm x 16.51cm) green-print rectangles and five 2½-in. (6.35cm) dark-blue-print squares together as shown. Iron. Sew the border to the top of the quilt center. Repeat to make the bottom border. Iron.

Middle Border

1. Sew four 2½-in. x 9-in. (6.35cm x 22.86cm) green-print rectangles, four 2½-in. (6.35cm) dark-blue-print squares, and one 2½-in. (6.35cm) green-print square together. Iron. Sew the border to one side of the quilt center. Repeat to make the other border. Iron.

2. Sew four 2½-in. x 6½-in. (6.35cm x 16.51cm) green-print rectangles, six 2½-in. (6.35cm) dark-blue-print squares and one 2½-in. (6.35cm) green-print square as shown. Iron. Sew the border to the top of the quilt center. Repeat to make the bottom border. Iron.

While a quilt is usually made to serve practical purposes, it can be displayed for its valuable needlework, each intricate detail representing the unique artistry and experiences of the quilter.

COLOR VARIATION

This little quilt has classic appeal when it is made in vintage-style fabrics. Available today in patterns reminiscent of the early '20s, '30s, '40s, and beyond, reproduction fabrics are designed in the colors and patterns of the past decades, each crisply printed on sturdy, dye-fast textiles. Make a quilt that has nostalgic style with none of the problems associated with antique fabrics.

Outer Border

1. Sew a 3½-in. x 48½-in. (8.89cm x 1.23m) medium-blue-print strip to each side of the quilt center. Iron.

2. Sew a 3½-in. (8.89cm) dark-blue-print square to each end of a 3½-in. x 38½-in. (8.89cm x 97.79cm) medium-blue print strip. Iron. Sew the strip to the top of the quilt. Iron. Repeat to make the bottom border.

FINISHING YOUR QUILT

1. Layer the quilt top, batting, and backing. See "Layering the Quilt," on page 118. Quilt as desired.

Whole Quilt Diagram

TIP

Scraps are treasures. Collect them a bit at a time, cutting 2¼-in. (5.72cm) squares from each as your scraps accumulate. Sew the squares into four-patch units, and when you have sewn 60 four-patch units, make a quilt. Piece them together to make one of your own design— or one in the style of "Giddy Walk."

pettiquilt junction

a quilt and pillowcases in grand style and "now" colors

An easy design and fabulous fabrics make this quilt a "must do" project. The queen-size quilt will add a sweep of color, pattern, and style to any bedroom. Inspired by the TV show *Petticoat Junction*, the quilt center is a cheerful mix of pink and green fabrics in whimsical prints. The quilt center is bordered in a fresh green-and-white-striped fabric and a narrow band in surprising purple, and is finished in an exuberant rose print that echoes the colors of all the fabrics. When the quilt is laid over a bed and accented with plump pillows that are enclosed in matching cases, the ensemble creates a look that is majestic and elegant.

skill level
Easy/Intermediate

full/queen size
82" x 93" (2.08m x 2.36m)

block size
12" (30.48cm) Finished

yardages
- ■ ⅝ yd. (0.57m) lt.-pink-print fabric #1
- ■ 1½ yds. (1.37m) lt.-pink-print fabric #2
- ■ ¾ yd. (0.69m) med.-pink-print fabric
- ■ 1¼ yds. (1.14m) dk.-pink-print fabric
- ■ ⅜ yd. (0.34m) green-print fabric
- ■ 1⅜ yds. (1.26m). purple-print fabric
- ■ 1¼ yds. (1.14m) green-stripe fabric
- ■ 1⅝ yds. (1.49m) floral-print fabric
- ■ 7⅜ yds. (6.74m) backing fabric, as desired
- ■ 88" x 100" (2.24m x 2.54m) batting
- ■ ½ yd. (0.46m) binding fabric, as desired

Quilt made by Velda Grubbs, machine-quilted by Sherry Massey

cutting table   Based on 42"-wide fabric

Fabric	Used for	FIRST CUT Number of pieces or crosswise strips	Cut size	SECOND CUT Number of pieces or crosswise strips	Cut size	THIRD CUT Number of pieces or crosswise strips	Cut size
Light-pink #1	Block A	4	4½" strips	30	4½" squares		
Light-pink #2	Block A	7	4½" strips	60	4½" squares		
	Block B	4	4⅞" strips	30	4⅞" squares		
Medium-pink print	Block B	5	4½" strips	45	4½" squares		
Dark-pink print	Block A and Block B	6	4⅞" strips	45	4⅞" squares		
	Block A	2	4½" strips	15	4½" squares		

cutting table (continued)

Fabric	Used for	FIRST CUT		SECOND CUT		THIRD CUT	
		Number of pieces or crosswise strips	Cut size	Number of pieces or crosswise strips	Cut size	Number of pieces or crosswise strips	Cut size
Green print	Block A	2	4⅞" strips	15	4⅞" squares		
Purple print 	Block B	4	4½" strips	30	4½" squares		
	Corner blocks	1	5⅞" strip	2	5⅞" squares		
				2	4⅞" squares		
	Border	8	2½" strips	Piece together and cut		2	2½" x 72½"
						2	2½" x 80½"
Green stripe 	Border	8	4½" strips	Piece together and cut			
		1	4⅞" strip	2	4⅞" squares		
Floral print 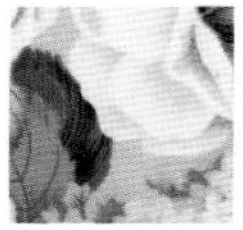	Corner blocks	1	5⅞" strip	2	5⅞" squares		
	Border	9	5½" strips	Piece together and cut		2	5½" x 72½"
						2	5½" x 84½"

Metric conversions for cutting table: 2½"(6.35cm) 4½"(11.43cm) 4⅞"(12.38cm) 5½"(13.97cm) 5⅞"(14.92cm) 42"(1.07m) 72½"(1.84m) 80½"(2.04m) 84½"(2.15m)

PETTIQUILT JUNCTION

BLOCK ASSEMBLY

Triangle Squares

1. Using a #2 pencil, mark a diagonal line on the back of a 4⅞-in. (12.38cm) green-print square. Layer the square on a 4⅞-in. (12.38cm) dark-pink square, right sides together. Sew a ¼-in. (0.64cm) seam on each side of the marked line.

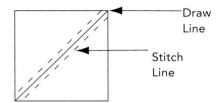

Draw Line

Stitch Line

2. Cut on the marked line. Iron. You will have two green-and-dark-pink-triangle squares. Repeat 14 times to make 30 green-and-dark-pink-triangle squares.

Block A

1. Sew one 4½-in. (11.43cm) light-pink-print #1 square, a 4½-in. (11.43cm) light-pink-print #2 square, and a green-and-dark-pink-triangle square together as shown. Iron. Repeat.

2. Sew two 4½-in. (11.43cm) light-pink-print #2 and one 4½-in. (11.43cm) dark-pink square together as shown. Iron.

3. Assemble Block A as shown. Repeat to make a total of 15 Block As.

Block B

1. Following the directions given to make triangle squares; make 60 light-pink-and-dark-pink-triangle squares using 30 4⅞-in. (12.38cm) light-pink #2 squares, and 30 4⅞-in. (12.38cm) dark-pink squares.

2. Sew a 4½-in. (11.43cm) medium-pink-print square, a light-pink-and-dark-pink-triangle square, and a 4½-in. (11.43cm) purple-print square together as shown. Iron. Repeat.

3. Sew two light-pink-and-dark-pink-triangle squares and a 4½-in. (11.43cm) medium-pink-print square together as shown. Iron.

4. Assemble Block B as shown. Iron. Repeat to make a total of 15 Block Bs.

QUILT ASSEMBLY

1. Assemble the quilt center five blocks across and six blocks down, alternating between Block As and Block Bs. See the "Whole Quilt Diagram" on page 69.

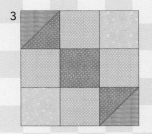

3

2

3

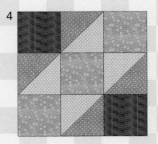

4

ADDING BORDERS

Inner Border

1. Referring to the directions for triangle squares on page 68, make four green-stripe-and-purple-triangle squares using two 4⅞-in. (12.38cm) green-stripe squares and two 4⅞-in. (12.38cm) purple-print squares. Iron.

2. Sew a 4½-in. x 72½-in. (11.43cm x 1.84m) green-stripe strip to each side of the quilt center. Iron.

3. Sew a green-stripe-and-purple-triangle square to each end of a 4½-in. x 60½-in. (11.43cm x 1.54m) green-stripe strip, making sure that the stripe runs in the same direction. Sew the strip to the top of the quilt. Iron. Repeat to make the bottom border.

Middle Border

1. Sew a 2½-in. x 80½-in. (6.35cm x 2.04m) purple-print strip to each side of the quilt. Iron.

2. Sew a 2½-in. x 72½-in. (6.35cm x 1.84m) purple-print strip to the top and bottom of the quilt. Iron.

Outer Border

1. Referring to the directions for triangle squares on page 68, make four floral-and-purple-triangle squares using two 5⅞-in. (14.92cm) floral-print squares and two 5⅞-in. (14.92cm) purple-print squares. Iron.

2. Sew a 5½-in. x 84½-in. (13.97 x 2.04m) floral-print strip to each side of the quilt. Iron.

3. Sew a floral-and-purple-triangle square to each end of one 5½-in. x 72½-in. (13.97cm x 1.84m) floral-print strip. Sew this strip to the top of the quilt. Iron. Repeat to make the bottom border.

FINISHING YOUR QUILT

1. Layer your quilt top, batting, and backing. See "Layering the Quilt," on page 118. Quilt as desired.

Whole Quilt Diagram

TIP

Quilts can be made in colors that suit your style preferences. Experiment by grouping paint chip samples together to see what combinations please you.

cutting table   Based on 42"-fabric

Fabric	Used for	FIRST CUT		SECOND CUT		THIRD CUT	
		Number of pieces or crosswise strips	Cut size	Number of pieces or crosswise strips	Cut size	Number of pieces or crosswise strips	Cut size
Main fabric	Case	2	25" strips	2	25" x 41" rectangles		
Floral fabric	Band	2	12½" strips	2	12½" x 41" rectangles		
Accent fabric	Trim	2	3" strips	2	3" x 41" strips		

Metric conversions for cutting table: 3"(7.62cm)   12½"(31.75cm)   25"(0.64m)   41"(1.04m)

TIP

"Dog ears" are points of fabric that extend beyond sewn edges, particularly with triangle-square units. Trim them even with the edge of the fabric before sewing the unit to the next piece.

COLOR VARIATION

Although the colorway of this variation on the featured pillowcase is very vivid, it conveys the bright palette of my take on "cottage style." The body of the pink pillowcase brings out the blue and yellow of the band. The colors would look great on a white-iron bed with these pillowcases, a matching quilt, and a blue gingham bed skirt.

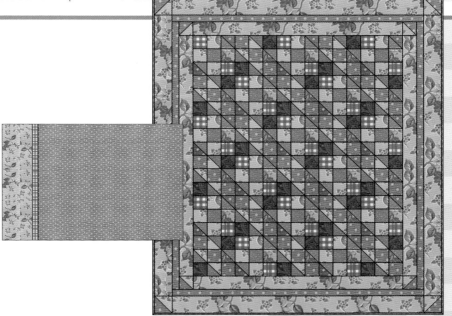

MATCHING PILLOWCASES

1. Fold one 25-in. x 41-in. (63.50cm x 1.04m) rectangle of the main fabric in half, right sides together. It will measure 20½ in. x 24½ in. (52.07cm x 62.23cm) after folding. Sew across one end and down one side. Trim off the corner where the seams cross as shown. Turn the case right side out. Iron.

2. Fold one 12½-in. x 41-in. (31.75cm x 1.04m) floral-fabric rectangle, right sides together, and stitch across the short ends to create a tube. Iron the seam open. Fold the tube in half, wrong sides together. Iron. Slip the tube inside the case, and pin along the raw edge, matching side seams.

3. Fold one 3-in. x 41-in. (7.62cm x 1.04m) accent-fabric strip, right sides together, and stitch across the short ends to make a tube. Iron the seam open. Slip the tube inside the case, right side facing the floral fabric, and pin along the raw edge, matching side seams. Stitch the layers together using a ½-in. (1.27cm) seam.

4. Fold and iron the accent trim in half, raw edges even. Fold under a ½-in. (1.27cm) hem along the raw edge. Iron the trim toward the lower edge of the case. Pin the hem to the case along the fold, trapping all raw edges in between. Or top stitch through all layers a scant ⅛-in. (0.32cm) from the seam line. Repeat for second pillowcase.

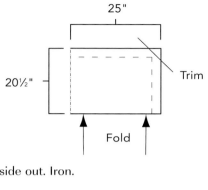

25"

20½"

Trim

Fold

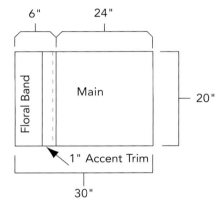

6" 24"

Floral Band

Main

20"

1" Accent Trim

30"

skill level

Easy

size

20" x 30" (50.80cm x 76.20cm)
(2 pillow cases)

yardages

- 1½ yds. (1.37m) main fabric
- ¾ yd. (0.69m) floral fabric
- ¼ yd.(0.23m) accent fabric

TIP

Striped fabrics can run either horizontally/ crosswise or vertically/ lengthwise from selvage to selvage. When purchasing a striped fabric for a project, check the direction of the stripes, as it may affect the amount of yardage needed.

come on
get scrappy

outdoor freshness using scraps
in faded colors

A s fresh and sweet as line-dried laundry, this quilt is made from a sun-bleached mix of pastels in small prints and solids. Each block of the quilt is configured from four three-piece squares that combine triangles and a band of snowy-white fabric. The secret to achieving the lattice-style pattern lies in the way each three-piece square is positioned. If you look at the "Whole Quilt Diagram" on page 77, you will see clearly how to assemble the blocks to make the pattern. In all cases, the quilt lends itself to a room painted white and washed in morning light. Add weathered furnishings to complete the look.

skill level
Advanced

throw size
52" x 72" (1.32m x 1.83m)

block size
5" (12.70cm)

yardages
- 2⅝ yds. (2.40m) white print
- 3¼ yds. (2.97m) assorted various prints
- ⅜ yd. (0.34m) pink-stripe print
- 3¼ yds. (2.97m) backing fabric, as desired.
- 58" x 78" (1.47m x 1.98m) batting
- ⅜ yd. (0.34m) binding fabric, as desired.

Quilt made by Velda Grubbs, machine-quilted by Sherry Massey

cutting chart Based on a 42"-wide fabric

Fabric	Used for	FIRST CUT Number of pieces or crosswise strips	Cut size	SECOND CUT Number of pieces or crosswise strips	Cut size	THIRD CUT Number of pieces or crosswise strips	Cut size
White print	Blocks	14	5½" strips	96	5½" squares		
	Inner blocks	6	2½" strips	Piece together and cut		2	2½" x 66½"
						2	2½" x 40½"
Assorted prints	Blocks	20	3⅞" strips	192	3⅞" squares	Note: Cut two of the same fabrics in increments.	
	Pieced border	13	2½" strips	116	2¼" x 4½" rectangles		
Pink-stripe print	Flange	6	1½" strips	Piece together and cut		2	2½" x 60½"
						2	2½" 40½"

Metric conversions for cutting table: 1½"(3.81cm) 2½"(6.35cm) 3⅞"(9.84cm) 4½"(11.43cm) 5½"(13.97cm) 40½"(1.03m) 42"(1.07m) 44½"(1.13m) 60½"(1.54m) 66½"(1.69m)

COME ON, GET SCRAPPY

BLOCK CONSTRUCTION

1. On wrong side of each 3⅞-in. (9.84cm) square, draw a pencil line diagonally from corner to corner.

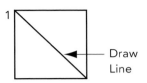

Draw Line

2. Place one 3⅞-in. (9.84cm) square in the corner of one 5½-in. (13.97cm) white square, with the drawn pencil line diagonally across the corner as shown. Sew on the drawn line. Trim off corner exactly ¼ in. (0.64cm) from the seam line just sewn.

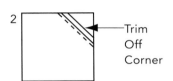

Trim Off Corner

Repeat to sew 5½-in. (13.97cm) white sqaure to the opposite corner. Press the corners outward to complete one block.

Repeat to make a total of 96 blocks.

QUILT ASSEMBLY

1. Following the "Whole Quilt Diagram" on page 77 for block placement, sew the blocks together in 12 rows of eight blocks each. Iron.

FLANGE

Note: The flange strip will be sandwiched between the quilt top and the inner border.

1. Fold one 1½-in. x 60½-in. (3.81cm x 1.54m) pink-stripe strip wrong sides together along the length of the strip. Iron.

2. Baste the longer flange strip to the long side of the quilt center, with all raw edges even. Repeat on the opposite side.

3. Fold the two 1½-in. x 40½-in. (3.81cm x 1.03m) pink-stripe strips for the top and bottom of the quilt as shown in step 1.

4. Baste these strips to the top and bottom of the quilt as shown in step 2. Note: Strips will overlap on the corners.

ADDING BORDERS

Inner Border

1. Sew a 2½-in. x 60½-in. (6.35cm x 1.54m) white strip to each long side of the quilt center, right sides facing, raw edges even, sandwiching the flange in between. Iron the white border toward the outer edge. Note: The folded edge of the flange will lay toward the quilt center.

2. Sew a 2½-in. x 40½-in. (6.35cm x 1.03m) white strip to the top and bottom of the quilt center. Iron the white border and the flange as directed in step 1 of flange.

Pieced Outer Border

1. Sew 33 2½-in. x 4½-in. (6.35cm x 11.43cm) rectangles together. Iron. Repeat. Sew the strips to the long sides of the quilt top.

2. Sew 27 2½-in. x 4½-in. (6.35cm x 11.43cm) rectangles together. Iron. Repeat. Sew the strips to the top and bottom of the quilt. Iron.

FINISHING THE QUILT

1. Layer the quilt top, batting, and backing. See "Layering the Quilt," on page 118. Quilt as desired.

COLOR VARIATION

Fabrics in rich jewel tones drastically change the look of the featured quilt from subtle to stand-out. When the quilt is placed in rooms whose furnishings are winter white, the quilt becomes the focal point of the room.

For a quilt with southwest style, choose fabrics in more bold colors — madder red, indigo, ochre, and green. More "modern" in sensibility, the quilt can be arranged over the arm of a couch.

Whole Quilt Diagram

TIP

To give this quilt an extra touch of sentimentality,
use scraps taken from old ties or pieces of a vintage dress.
Make a keepsake for your daughter using swatches of her favorite
childhood dresses or blankets. Each glimpse of
the quilt will bring back pleasant
memories.

table scraps

a treasure from scraps

skill level
Easy

table runner
21¼" x 63½" (61.60cm x 1.61m)

block size
5" (12.70cm)

yardages
- ¾ yd. (0.69m) white print
- 1 yd. (0.91m) various prints
- 2 yds. (1.83m) backing fabric, as desired
- 27" x 70" batting (68.58cm x 1.78m)
- ⅜ yd. (0.34m) binding, as desired

Quilt made by Velda Grubbs, machine-quilted by Sherry Massey

Turn your favorite scraps of fabric into something special, such as this table runner, aptly called "Table Scraps." The pieced runner features pastel plaids and solids in a triangle pattern and a leafgreen binding that pulls the pattern together. Although we used our scraps from "Get Scrappy," on page 72, to make this runner, you can choose any scraps that appeal to you. When your runner is finished, display it everyday on a dresser, or move it to a place of more prominence when special occasions arise. The beauty and aritstry of this project will add a unique touch to any space.

cutting table — Based on a 42"-wide fabric

Fabric	Used for	FIRST CUT Number of pieces or crosswise strips	FIRST CUT Cut size	SECOND CUT Number of pieces or crosswise strips	SECOND CUT Cut size	THIRD CUT Number of pieces or crosswise strips	THIRD CUT Cut size
White print	Blocks	7	3½" strips	78	3½" squares		
Various prints	Blocks	7	3½" strips	78	3½" squares		
	Side triangles	1	8¾" strip	3	8¾" squares	12 triangles	

Metric conversions for cutting table: 3½"(8.89cm) 8¾"(22.23cm) 42"(1.07m)

TABLE SCRAPS

BLOCK CONSTRUCTION

1. On the wrong side of each 3½-in. (8.89cm) white square, draw a pencil line diagonally from corner to corner.

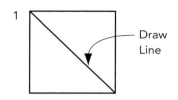

Draw Line

2. Layer one 3½-in. (8.89cm) white square on top of a 3½-in. (8.89cm) various-print square with right sides facing. Sew a ¼-in.-wide (0.64cm) seam on each side of the drawn line.

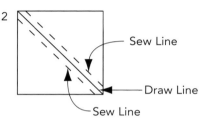

Sew Line

Draw Line

Sew Line

3. Cut the layers apart along the drawn pencil line to make two-triangle squares. Repeat to make a total of 156 triangle squares.

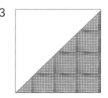

4. Sew four of the completed triangle squares together to make a pinwheel block as shown. Iron. Trim to make a 5½-in. (13.97cm) block if necessary, being careful to keep the triangle points exactly at the corners. Repeat to make a total of 39 blocks.

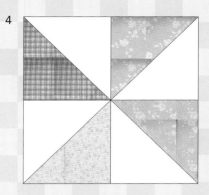

5. To make side triangles, draw intersecting diagonal lines on the wrong side of each 8¾-in. (22.23cm) square. Cut along the lines to make four triangles. Repeat three times for a total of 12 side triangles. Referring to the "Construction Diagram," on page 83, sew the pinwheel blocks and the side triangles together to complete the table runner.

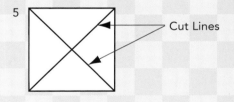

Cut Lines

FINISHING THE RUNNER

1. Layer the runner top, batting, and backing. See "Layering the Quilt," on page 118. Quilt as desired.

TIP

It is very helpful to refer to the "Construction Diagram" on page 83 before assembling the table runner. The diagram clearly shows how to lay out the pattern.

COLOR VARIATION

gain, the richer jewel tone colors create an entirely new feel in this conglomerate of scraps. These lustrous colors are a great alternative for this table runner. "Table Scraps" is a design perfectly suited to any table that you choose.

TIP

If you have leftover fabric from a window treament, use it to make a small lap throw. Upolstery-weight fabric has heft and makes for a cozy coverlet. Be certain to match the thread to the fabric content of your project.

When perfectionism beguiles you, ignore it; if encouraged, it will be the greatest obstacle to beginning your work.

Construction Diagram

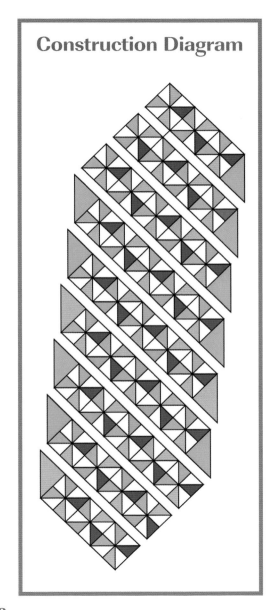

TIP

Bulk often builds up at the intersection of several seams, especially in the "Pinwheel" pattern where several points come together at a center. To help ease the layers of fabric at the intersection so that they lay flat, turn the block to the wrong side, and remove a few stitches along the seam, leaving the last stitch intact. Iron the seams flat so that they radiate like a fan in a clockwise orientation. This should help reduce the bulk.

worth repeating

simply playful fun

It's so easy! It's so easy! The declaration is certainly worth repeating because this delightful quilt, aptly named "Worth Repeating," is so simple to make. In fact, it is a perfect quilt for beginners. Squares in a similar colorway are sewn together to make a strip; 16 strips are sewn together to make the quilt center; borders are added to all four sides. With careful attention to your fabric choices and the block placement, you can achieve a "gingham" look like that shown here. The quilt is a versatile decorating element. It can be laid over a bed or on a little side table to add a burst of unexpected color.

skill level
Easy

toddler size
51" x 60" (1.30m x 1.52m)

block size
3" (7.62cm)

yardages
- ¼ yd. (0.23m) lt.-blue and med.-blue print fabrics
- ¼ yd. (0.23m) lt.-yellow and med.-yellow print fabrics
- ¼ yd. (0.23m) lt.-purple and med.-purple print fabrics
- ¼ yd. (0.23m) lt.-orange and med.-orange print fabrics
- 1 yd. (0.91m) lt.-pink print fabric
- ½ yd. (0.46m) med.-pink print fabric
- ¼ yd. (0.23m) lt.-green print fabric
- ⅜ yd. (0.34m) med.-green print fabric
- 3¼ yds. (2.97m) backing fabric, as desired
- 57" x 66" batting (1.45m x 1.68m)
- ⅜ yd. (0.34m) binding fabric, as desired

Quilt made and machine-quilted by Sherry Massey

cutting table Based on a 42"-wide fabric

Fabric	Used for	FIRST CUT — Number of pieces or crosswise strips	Cut size	SECOND CUT — Number of pieces or crosswise strips	Cut size	THIRD CUT — Number of pieces or crosswise strips	Cut size
Light-blue and medium-blue prints	Blocks	2 of each print	3½" strips				
Light-yellow and medium-yellow prints	Blocks	2 of each print	3½" strips				
Light-purple and medium-purple prints	Blocks	2 of each print	3½" strips				
Light-orange and medium-orange prints	Blocks	2 of each print	3½" strips				
Light-pink print	Blocks	3	3½" strips				
	Border	5	3½" strips	Piece together and cut		2	3½" x 45½"
						2	3½" x 54½"
Medium-pink print	Blocks	3	3½" strips				
	Corner blocks	1	3½" strip	4	3½" squares		
Light-green print	Blocks	2	3½" strips				
	Borders	5	3½" strips	Piece together and cut		2	3½" x 39½"
						2	3½" x 48½"
Medium-green print	Blocks	2	3½" strips				
	Corner blocks	1	3½" strip	4	3½" squares		

Metric conversions for cutting chart: 3½"(8.89cm) 39½"(1.00m) 42"(1.07m) 45½"(1.16m) 48½"(1.23m) 54½"(1.38m)

WORTH REPEATING

QUILT ASSEMBLY

1. Sew together lengthwise one 3½-in. (8.89cm) light-pink print strip and one 3½-in. (8.89cm) medium-pink print crosswise strip as shown. Iron the seam open. Repeat two times to make a total of three pink-strip sets.

2. From the strip sets, cut 24 3½-in.-wide (8.89cm) strip set segments as shown.

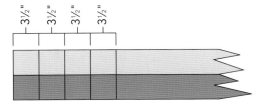

3. Following steps 1–2, make two blue-strip sets, two green-strip sets, two yellow strip sets, two purple-strip sets, and two orange-strip sets. From each strip, cut 16 3-in.-wide (8.89cm) strip set segments.

4. Sew eight pink-strip set segments together as shown. Iron. Repeat twice to make a total of three pink rows.

5. Following step 4, make two blue rows, two green rows, two yellow rows, two purple rows, and two orange rows.

6. Sew the rows togethers vertically, starting with a pink row. See the "Whole Quilt Diagram" on page 89. Iron the seams open.

Inner Border

1. Sew a 3½-in. x 48 ½-in. (8.89cm x 1.23m) light-green strip to each side of the quilt center. Iron.

2. Sew a 3½-in. (8.89cm) medium-pink print square to each end of a 3½-in. x 39½- in. (8.89cm x 1.00m) light-green strip. Iron the seams open. Sew the strip to the top of the quilt center. Iron. Repeat to make and sew a strip to the bottom.

Outer Border

1. Sew a 3½-in. x 54½-in. (8.89cm x 1.38m) light-pink print to each side of the quilt center. Iron.

2. Sew a 3½-in. (8.89cm) medium-green print square to each end of a 3½-in. x 45½-in. (8.89cm x 1.16m) light-pink print strip. Sew the strip to the top of the quilt center. Iron. Repeat to make and sew a strip to the bottom border.

FINISHING

1. Layer the quilt top, batting, and backing. See "Layering the Quilt," on page 118.

TIP

Ironing is an essential part of making a quilt. After machine-stiching your fabric strips together, remember to iron the seams open so that they lay flat. If you do this, your quilting stiches will be neater and easier to sew.

The soft pastel
prints of
this variation of
"Worth Repeating"
show how a change
in fabric alters the
sensibility of the
quilt from one that
is energetic to one
that is calm.

COLOR VARIATION

S weet and cozy, the color palette of this beautiful variation of "Worth Repeating" goes nicely in a baby's nursery. The pattern is easy to create and can be made in any colors that appeal to you.

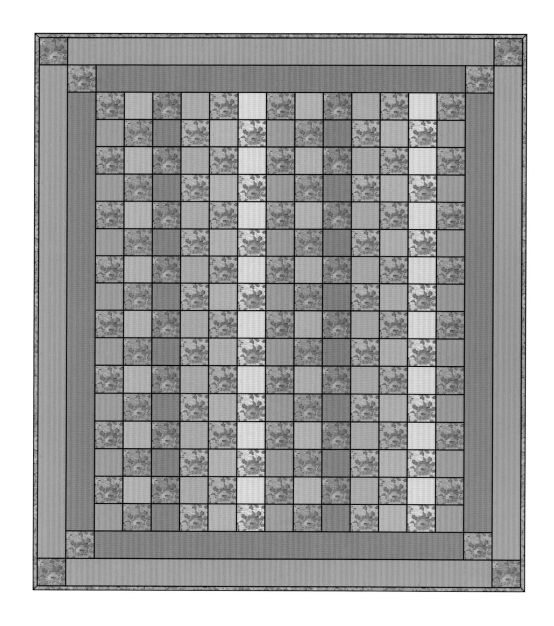

Using Scraps of Batting

To use pieces of leftover batting that are not large enough for a whole quilt-project, first straighten, or "square up," the edges of the batting scraps. Abut two edges together, without overlapping them, and hand sew them along the adjacent edges using a threaded needle and the whipstich. If you prefer to use a sewing machine, set the stitch guide to the widest zigzag stitch, and sew the pieces together, letting the needle fall on each side of abutted edges. Practice the sewing technique on several scraps, if desired.

Whole Quilt Diagram

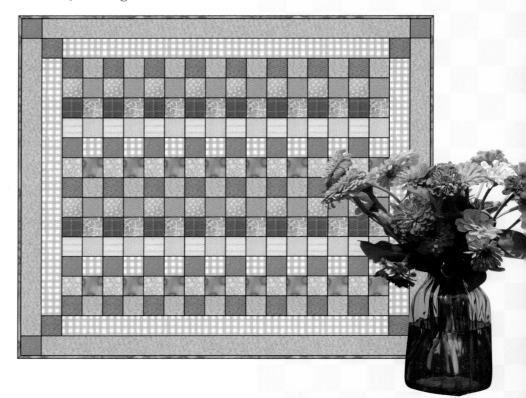

sweet as cotton candy

domestic confection

Nothing says a "good time" at the fair like the Tilt-A-Whirl, corn dogs, and cotton candy, especially cotton candy with its paper cone overflowing with spun sugar. It is guaranteed to light up a little one's eyes, as will this quilt, "Sweet as Cotton Candy." Making the quilt is as easy as sewing half-square triangles together (to make the top) and adding a few borders (to the sides) to create a quilt in a pieced confection of pastel pinks and blues. Suited to a crib size, the quilt can also be adapted for use as a wall-hanging in a child's room, or it can be used as a cozy coverlet in the family room.

skill level
Easy

crib size
44" x 54" (1.12m x 1.37m)

block size
10" (25.40cm)

yardages
- ⅝ yd. (0.57m) lt.-blue print
- ⅝ yd. (0.57m) med.-blue print
- ⅞ yd. (0.80m) med.-pink print
- ⅝ yd. (0.57m) white-floral print
- ⅜ yd. (0.34m) lt.-pink print
- 2⅞ yds. (2.63m) backing fabric, as desired
- 50" x 60" batting (1.27m x 1.52m)
- ⅜ yd. (0.34m) binding fabric, as desired

Quilt made by Dianna Olson, machine-quilted by Sherry Massey

cutting table — Based on a 42"-wide fabric

Fabric	Used for	FIRST CUT Number of pieces or crosswise strips	Cut size	SECOND CUT Number of pieces or crosswise strips	Cut size	THIRD CUT Number of pieces or crosswise strips	Cut size
Light-blue print 	Blocks	3	5⅞" strips	20	5⅞" squares		
Medium-blue print 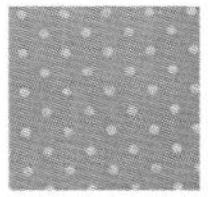	Blocks	2	5⅞" strips	10	5⅞" squares		
	Border	5	1½" strips	Piece together and cut		2	1½" x 44½"
						2	1½" x 52½"
Medium-pink print	Blocks	3	5⅞" strips	20	5⅞" squares		
	Border	5	1½" strips	Piece together and cut		2	1½" x 42½"
						2	1½" x 50½"
White print 	Blocks	3	5⅞" strips	20	5⅞" squares		
Light-pink print 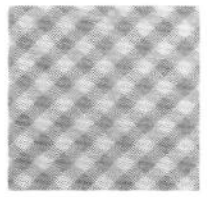	Blocks	2	5⅞" strips	10	5⅞" squares		

Metric conversions for cutting chart: 1½"(3.81cm)   5⅞"(14.92cm)   42"(1.07m)   42½"(1.08m)   44½"(1.13m)   50½"(1.28m)   52½"(1.33m)

SWEET AS COTTON CANDY

BLOCK ASSEMBLY

Triangle Squares

1. Using a #2 pencil, draw a diagonal line on the back of a 5⅞-in. (14.92cm) white-print square. Layer the 5⅞-in. (14.92cm) white-print square and a 5⅞-in. (14.92cm) light-blue-print square, right sides together. Sew a ¼-in. (0.64cm) seam on each side of the marked line.

Draw Line

Stitch Line

2. Cut on the marked line. Open up the white-and-light-blue-triangle square. Iron.

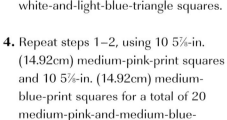

3. Repeat steps 1–2, using the remaining 19 5⅞-in. (14.92cm) white-print squares and 19 5⅞-in. (14.92cm) light-blue-print squares for a total of 40 white-and-light-blue-triangle squares.

4. Repeat steps 1–2, using 10 5⅞-in. (14.92cm) medium-pink-print squares and 10 5⅞-in. (14.92cm) medium-blue-print squares for a total of 20 medium-pink-and-medium-blue-triangle squares.

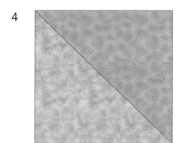

5. Repeat steps 1–4, using 10 5⅞-in. (14.92cm) medium-pink-print squares and 10 5⅞-in. (14.92cm) light-pink squares for a total of 20 medium-pink-and-light-pink-triangle squares.

6. Using two white-and-light-blue-triangle squares, one medium-pink-and-medium-blue-triangle square, and one medium-pink-and-light-pink-triangle square, assemble the block.

QUILT ASSEMBLY

1. Sew together four blocks across and five blocks down to make the quilt center.

ADDING BORDERS

Inner Border

1. Sew a 1½-in. x 50½-in. (3.81cm x 1.28m) medium-pink print to each side of the quilt center. Iron.

2. Sew one 1½-in. x 42½-in. (3.81cm x 1.08m) medium-pink print to the top and the bottom of the quilt center. Iron.

Outer Border

1. Sew a 1½-in. x 52½-in. (3.81cm x 1.33m) medium-blue strip to each side of the quilt center. Iron.

2. Sew a 1½-in. x 44½-in. (3.81cm x 1.13m) medium-blue strip to the top and the bottom of the quilt center. Iron.

FINISHING YOUR QUILT

1. Layer your quilt top, batting, and backing. Quilt as desired.

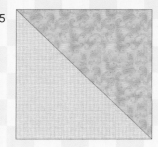

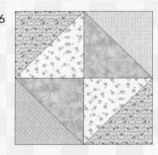

As lively as a circus, this variation of "Sweet as Cotton Candy" is worked in happy crayon colors, making it the perfect quilt to hang in a young child's room.

COLOR VARIATION

Here is a fun color option for this quick little crib quilt using "brights." While the featured quilt is shown in colors that might be described as feminine, sweet, and pretty, this color variation has a more masculine sensibility. Another design approach is to make the quilt in different shades of one color for a quilt with more subtle style.

Whole Quilt Diagram

Quilt Top Tip

Lay all the blocks on a flat surface, following the "Whole Quilt Diagram." Make a stack of blocks for each row, placing the last block in each row first and the first block last. Label each stack. To assemble each row, lay the first two blocks together, right sides facing. Pin and sew one side. Open the pair. Pin the third block, right side down, on the second block, aligning the edges. Sew one side to make a three-block row. Continue to sew the remaining blocks in the stack to make one row. Repeat the steps to sew the remaining stacks. To make the quilt top, sew the adjacent rows together.

TIP

Pieced triangle squares are made by joining two triangles of fabric along their diagonal edges to form a square. When the triangle squares are arranged, they can produce unique optical illusions and such creative variations as starflowers, birds, and geometric patterns.

wing ding

happy colors and a twist of fun

T his quilt is a "party waiting to happen," and similar to preparing for a festive occasion, it will take a little more time and effort to make before you can enjoy it. However, when you see the bright colors coming together in blocks and the blocks being transformed into a quilt, you will be rewarded with a cheerful design that is as much fun to look at as it was to make. The beautiful colors make a bold statement and create a feel-good vibe that will brighten anyone's day.

Invite your friends over for a "Wing Ding" quilting party. See how the style and personality of this quilt adds to the fun.

skill level
Intermediate

queen size
88¾" x 111½" (2.25m x 2.83m)

block size
15"(38.10cm)

yardages
- 5¾ yds. (5.26m) pink print
- 2¼ yds. (2.06m) green print
- 2⅛ yds. (1.94m) white print
- 7⅞ yds. (7.20m) backing fabric, as desired
- 92" x 114" (2.34m x 2.90m) batting
- ¾ yd. (0.69m) binding fabric, as desired

Quilt made by Dianna Olson, machine-quilted by Sherry Massey

cutting table Based on a 42"-wide fabric

Fabric	Used for	FIRST CUT		SECOND CUT		THIRD CUT	
		Number of pieces or crosswise strips	Cut size	Number of pieces or crosswise strips	Cut size	Number of pieces or crosswise strips	Cut size
Pink print	Side triangles	4	22½" strips	4	22½" squares	Cut twice diagonally	
		From remaining width cut:		24	6½" squares	For Block A	
	Block A	10	6½" strips	56	6½" squares		
	Block B	13	3½" strips				
Green print	Block A	7	3½" strips	20	3½" squares		
	Block B	12	3½" strips				
White print	Block A	14	3½" strips	160	3½" squares		
		7	3½" strips				

Metric conversions for cutting table: 3½"(8.89cm) 6½"(16.51cm) 22½"(57.15cm) 42"(1.07m)

WING DING

QUILT ASSEMBLY

Block A

1. Using a #2 pencil, draw a diagonal line on the back of two 3½-in. (8.89cm) white-print squares.

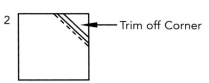

1

Drawn Line

2. Place one 3½-in. (8.89cm) white-print square in the corner of a 6½-in. (16.51cm) pink-print square, with the marked line diagonally across the corner. Sew on the marked line. Trim off the corner ¼- in. (0.64cm) from the seam line just sewn. Iron the corners outward.

2

Trim off Corner

3. Repeat at the opposite corner of the pink-print square. Iron the corners outward.

4. Repeat three times for a total of four Block As.

5. Sew together lengthwise one 3½-in. (8.89cm) green-print strip and one 3½-in. (8.89cm) white-print strip. Iron. Repeat six more times to make a total of six strip sets.

5

6. From the strip sets, cut 80 3½-in. (8.89cm) strip-set segments.

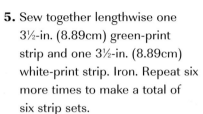

6

7. Sew together four Block As, four strip-set segments, and one 3½-in. (8.89cm) green-print square, as shown. Iron.

8. Repeat 19 times to make a total of 20 Block As.

Block B

1. Sew together three 3½-in. (8.89cm) pink-print strips and two 3½-in. (8.89cm) green-print strips as shown. Iron. Repeat two more times to make a total of three strip sets.

1

2. Cut the strip sets into 36 3½-in. (8.89cm) A strip-set segments.

2

3. Following steps 1 and 2, sew together three green-print and two 3½-in. (8.89cm) pink-print strips. Iron. Repeat to make a total of two strip sets.

4. Cut the strip sets into 24 3½-in. (8.89cm) B strip-set segments.

5. Assemble Block B as shown, using three A strip-set segments and two B strip-set segments.

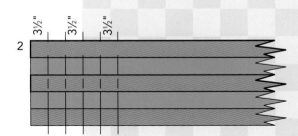

7

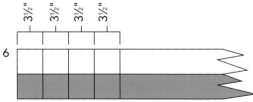

Cues for the color that you choose for your quilts can come from anywhere—the landscape, the pattern on a favorite chair, or your own personal preferences. It is always important that the colors appeal to you.

COLOR VARIATION

Choose a red that has rich undertones, and modify the background fabrics to make this variation on the featured quilt. The new colors shift the focal point, giving the pattern a whole new look. Or key the fabric colors to those in your room to make a quilt that coordinates with the furnishings.

6. Repeat 11 times for a total of 12 Block Bs.

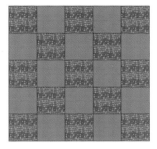

QUILT ASSEMBLY

1. Referring to the "Construction Diagram," assemble the rows as shown. Cut two 22½-in. (57.15cm) triangles in half as shown. Use these triangles as corner triangles. Iron.

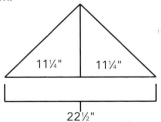

FINISHING YOUR QUILT

1. Layer the quilt top, batting, and backing. See "Layering the Quilt," on page 118. Quilt as desired.

Construction Diagram

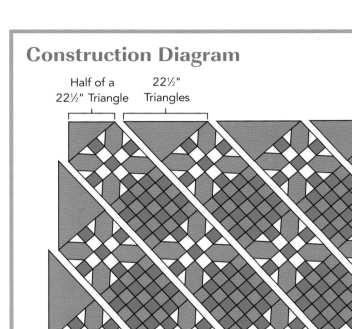

Half of a 22½" Triangle

22½" Triangles

we
all scream

add flavor to your quilting

I scream, you scream, "We All Scream...." for ice cream! The old-fashioned cheer is usually associated with the delicious frozen confection and the ringing bells on the ice-cream trucks that rolled through neighborhoods in the '50s and '60s. The light-hearted joy of that time is echoed in this quilt designed with fabrics using ice-cream motifs and colors—rich chocolate brown, French vanilla, and strawberry—that are played against a bright-blue border more reminiscent of the fantasy hues of ice pops. Combined in blocks, squares, and triangles, the colors work together to carry out the flavor of this sweet quilt.

skill level
Easy/ Intermediate

wall hanging size
48" x 48" (1.22m x 1.22m)

block size
12" (30.48cm)

yardages
- ½ yd. (0.46m) ice cream print fabric (focus fabric)
- ¾ yd. (0.69m) blue-print fabric
- ⅜ yd. (0.34m) green-print fabric
- ½ yd. (0.46m) yellow-print fabric
- ¾ yd. (0.69m) pink-print fabric
- ¼ yd. (0.23m) brown-print fabric
- 3 yds. (2.74m) backing fabric, as desired
- 54" x 54" (1.37m x 1.37m) batting
- ⅜ yd. (0.34m) binding fabric, as desired

Quilt made by Velda Grubbs, machine-quilted by Sherry Massey

cutting table   Based on a 42"-wide fabric

Fabric	Used for	FIRST CUT Number of pieces or crosswise strips	FIRST CUT Cut size	SECOND CUT Number of pieces or crosswise strips	SECOND CUT Cut size	THIRD CUT Number of pieces or crosswise strips	THIRD CUT Cut size
Focus	Blocks	2	6½" strips	9	6½" squares		
Blue print	Blocks	6	2" strips				
	Border	4	3" strips	2	3" x 36½"		
				2	3" x 41½"		
Green print	Blocks	6	2" strips				
Yellow print	Blocks	7	2" strips	144	2" squares		
Pink print	Blocks	3	3½" strips	36	3½" squares		
	Border	5	3" strips	Piece together and cut		2	3" x 43½"
						2	3" x 48½"
Brown print	Border	5	1½" strips	Piece together and cut		2	1½" x 41½"
						2	1½" x 43½"

Metric conversions for cutting table: 1½"(3.81cm)   2"(5.08cm)   3"(7.62cm)   3½"(8.89cm)   6½"(16.51cm)   36½"(0.93m)   41½"(1.05m)   42"(1.07cm)   43½"(1.10m)   48½"(1.23m)

WE ALL SCREAM

BLOCK CONSTRUCTION

Square in a Square:

1. Using a #2 pencil, draw a diagonal line on the wrong side of four 2-in. (5.08cm) yellow-print squares as shown.

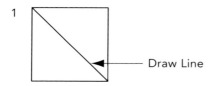
Draw Line

2. Position one 2-in. (5.08cm) yellow-print square on one corner of a 3½-in. (8.89cm) pink-print square, right sides together. Stitch on the marked line, and trim off the corner leaving a ¼-in. (0.64cm) seam allowance. Iron the triangle outward.

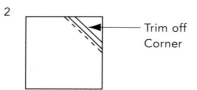
Trim off Corner

3. Repeat step 2 to stitch one yellow-print square to the corner opposite the corner sewn in step 2. Trim and iron the corner outward. Stitch the other two yellow-print squares to the remaining corners. Trim and iron the corners outward.

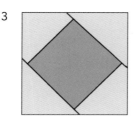

4. Repeat 35 times for a total of 36 pink-and-yellow-print "square-in-a-square" units.

Strip Sets:

1. Sew a 2-in. (5.08cm) blue-print strip and a 2-in. (5.08cm) green-print strip together. Iron.

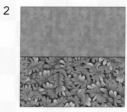

2. Cut the strip into six 6½-in. (16.51cm) strip set segments.

3. Repeat with the remaining five 2-in. (5.08cm) blue-print strips and five green-print strips. From the strip sets, cut 30 6½-in. (16.51cm) strip set segments, for a total of 36 segments.

Block Construction:

1. Sew a pink-and-yellow-print "square in a square" to each end of a blue-and-green-print strip set segment as shown. Iron. Repeat.

2. Sew a blue-and-green-print strip set segment to each side of a 6½-in. (16.51cm) focus fabric square. Iron.

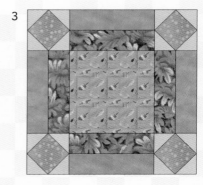

3. Assemble the block as shown. Iron.

COLOR VARIATION

Change the style and sensibility of the featured quilt from whimsical to Country French by substituting solid and print fabrics in azur blue, ochre, and dark red. The earthy but elegant tones will evoke the countryside of the south of France.

Use fabrics in richly contrasting colors to highlight small shapes.

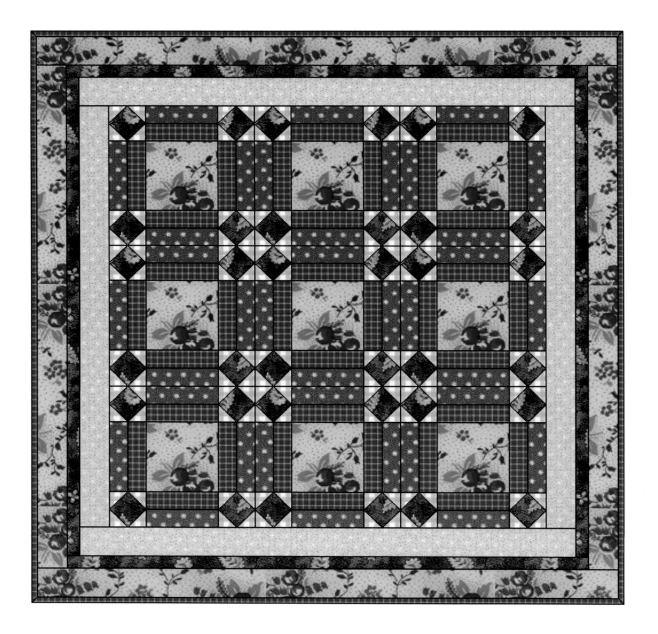

QUILT ASSEMBLY

1. Assemble the quilt center three blocks across and three blocks down. See the "Whole Quilt Diagram," at right. Iron.

ADDING BORDERS

Inner Border

1. Sew a 3" x 36½" (7.62cm x 0.93m) blue-print strip to each side of quilt center. Iron.

2. Sew a 3" x 41½" (7.62cm x 1.05m) blue-print strip to the top and bottom of the quilt center. Iron.

Middle Border

1. Sew a 1½" x 41½" (3.81cm x 1.05m) brown-print strip to each side of the quilt center. Iron.

2. Sew a 1½" x 43½" (3.81cm x 1.10m) brown-print strip to the top and bottom of the quilt center. Iron.

Outer Border

1. Sew a 3" x 43½" (7.62cm x 1.10m) pink-print strip to each side of the quilt. Iron.

2. Sew a 3" x 48½" (7.62cm x 1.23m) pink-print strip to the top and bottom. Iron.

Whole Quilt Diagram

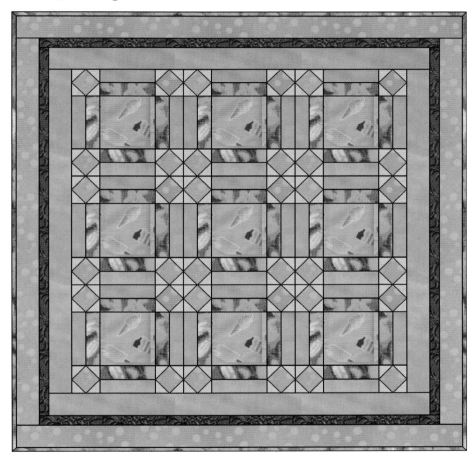

FINISHING YOUR QUILT

1. Layer your quilt top, batting, and backing. See "Layering your Quilt," on page 118. Quilt as desired.

TIP

Finding great fabric on the Internet is fast and easy. For fabric with ice cream motifs, start your search by using "fabric" and you will see a vast number of manufacturers listed. Refine your search by adding "ice-cream-print fabric." For fabrics with particular fiber contents, enter the name of the fiber, say, 100% cotton fabric. For fabulous reproductions, enter "reproduction fabric."

quilting
basics

all you need to know to quilt like a pro

Quilting is so much fun that you will be inspired to begin any one of the beautiful quilts included in "The Collection." Before you begin, however, it is recommended that you read through this useful section to familiarize yourself with the tools and guidelines needed to ensure a satisfying and productive experience that results in a quilt that you are proud to use, display, or give to family and friends.

tools

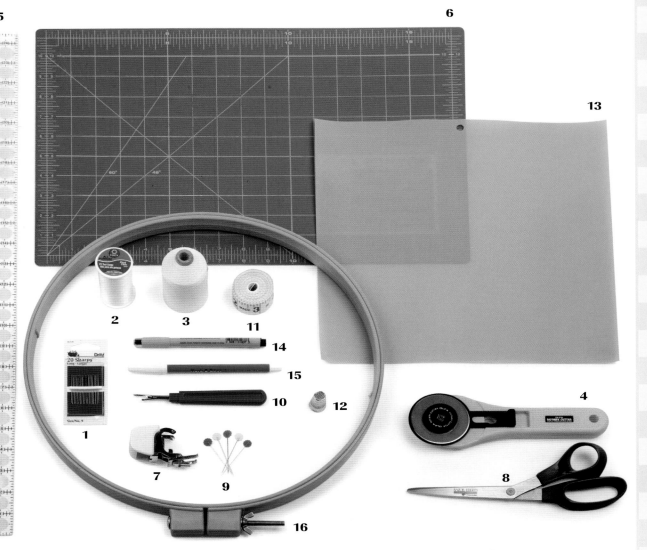

Having the right tools handy will make your quilting experiences more efficient and enjoyable. These are the essential tools you will need:

NEEDLES

1. **Betweens** (short, strong; size 8 recommended for beginners)
   Sharps (longer, thinner; for basting and hand sewing)

THREAD

2. **All-purpose sewing**
3. **Quilting**

ROTARY CUTTER, RULER, AND MAT

4. **Rotary cutter:** 1.77" or 2.36" (4.50cm or 6.00cm)
5. **Acrylic ruler:** 6" x 24" (15.24cm x 60.96cm)
6. **Self-healing cutting mat:** 18" x 24" (45.72cm x 60.96cm)

ADDITIONAL TOOLS

7. **Walking foot for sewing machine**
8. **Scissors**
9. **Flat-head quilting pins**
10. **Seam ripper**
11. **Tape measure**
12. **Thimble**
13. **Plastic template material**
14. **Permanent fine-point marker**
15. **Marker with washable-ink**
16. **Quilting hoop**

preparing the fabric

1. The fabric requirements listed for each project are based on 42-in.-wide (1.07m) fabric. Fabrics that are less than 42-in.-wide (1.07m) may require additional yardage.

2. Use fabrics that are easy to work with, choosing 100% cotton fabrics whenever possible.

3. Shrinkage varies from fabric to fabric. For best results, pre-wash all fabrics using a mild detergent. Do not use fabric softener.

4. Dry the fabric. Iron it before starting your quilt project, using a light spray starch to restore the crisp finish to the fabric.

5. If you plan to make crosswise strips from your fabric, fold the fabric in half, selvage to selvage, then fold it in half again to make four layers, keeping the edges even. The fabric is now ready to cut using a rotary cutter and a ruler.

TIP

Pre-washing your fabrics and storing them properly is very important. Preparing your fabrics means that they will be ready to use when you begin your next project.

cutting fabric strips using a rotary cutter

CAUTION: Always roll the cutter away from your body, and close the guard on the cutter blade after each cut to avoid serious injury.

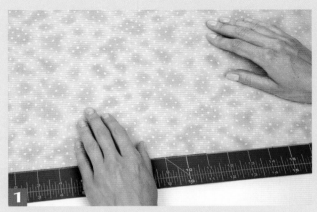

1 Fold the fabric, following step 5 on page 110. Place the fold of the fabric closest to your body and along one horizontal line on the lower section of the mat.

2 Square up the fabric. Lay the ruler over the left side of the fabric as shown, aligning the edge of the ruler with a vertical line on the mat. Place the rotary cutter at the lower right edge of the ruler, and roll it away from you to cut through all fabric layers. (See note.)

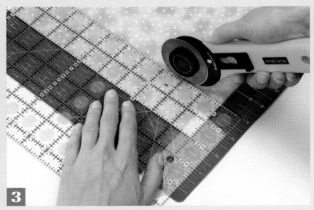

3 To cut a 2-in.-wide (5.08cm) strip, position the ruler over the edge of fabric, aligning the 2-in.-width (5.08cm) measurement on the ruler with the cut edge of the fabric as shown. Hold the ruler firmly with your left hand. Cut the strip along the right side of the ruler using the rotary cutter.

4 Repeat steps 2–3 to cut the desired number of strips. If you wish to cut the strips into smaller units, such as squares, repeat the steps.

Note: The steps are written for a right-handed person; if you are left-handed, reverse the directions.

sewing fabric pieces

Precise cutting, piecing, and ironing are all important to ensure that your quilt top will go together neatly and accurately.

PIECING: SEWING TWO PIECES

Note: Practice sewing ¼-in.-wide (0.64cm) seams until you achieve consistent results.

Place the pieces together with their right sides facing and raw edges even. Use a pin to secure them along one side.

Slip the pieces under the presser foot, and sew a ¼-in.-wide (0.64cm) seam, removing the pins as you work.

Note: You can buy a "¼-in. foot" (0.64cm) for the sewing machine that near-guarantees perfect seams.

CHAIN PIECING: SEWING TWO-PIECE PAIRS

Chain piecing allows you to piece more quickly.

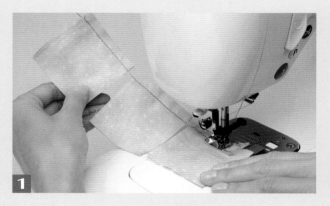

Feed one two-piece pair into the machine, sewing a ¼-in.-wide (0.64cm) seam along one pinned side. Assemble another two-piece pair, and feed it into the machine. Continue to sew pairs, making a "chain" of two-piece pairs.

After making a chain with the desired number of two-piece pairs, cut the threads between the pairs. Iron each pair.

sewing fabric pieces

A "strip set" is composed of two or more fabric strips that are sewn together to make one unit. Sew two strips together. When joining each strip thereafter, sew the seam in the opposite direction from that used in the previous strip to avoid stretching and distorting the fabric.

SEWING STRIP SETS

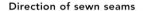

Direction of sewn seams

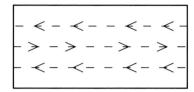

Front

Back

SEWING ACROSS INTERSECTIONS

1 Sew two two-piece pairs as directed on page 112, "Piecing: Sewing Two Pieces."

2 Iron the seam allowance toward one side so that the light-colored seam overlaps the dark-colored seam.

3 Lay the two-piece pairs on a flat surface with the seam allowances facing in opposite directions as shown.

4 Lay the two-piece pairs together with their right sides facing and their seams matching as shown.

5 Use a flat-head quilting pin to secure the pair with their seams matching and in the direction of the darker fabric.

6 Machine-stitch a ¼-in.-wide (0.64cm) seam to make a four-patch unit.

SEWING SHARP POINTS

Turn the unit to the wrong side. To sew a sharp point, use the sewing machine to stitch a line across the "X," sewing a scant ¹⁄₁₆ in. (0.16cm) above the center of the "X" formed by the seams.

1

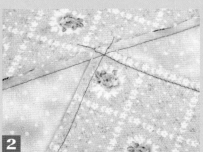

2

making a template

Templates are great tools to use when marking pattern pieces on fabric. Made from thin plastic, they ensure that the pattern lines marked on the fabric are consistent and precise. Templates are commonly used for pieced and appliqué quilts because their pieces often have curved lines that cannot be cut easily with a rotary cutter. Sturdy cardboard may also be used to make a template.

1

To make a template, lay a copy of the pattern on the plastic, and trace around it, using a permanent marker.

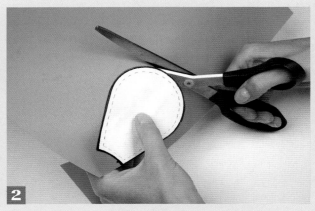

2

Cut along the marked line using sharp scissors to make one plastic template of your pattern piece.

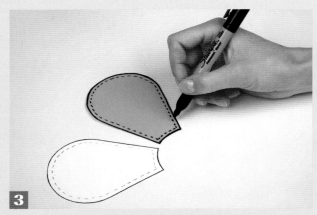

3

Lay the template over the paper-pattern piece and trace all the sewing directions and guides on the template using the marker.

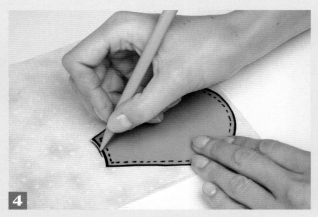

4

Lay the template on the wrong side of the fabric and use a sharp pencil to trace around the perimeter of the template. Mark the sewing directions by "eye."

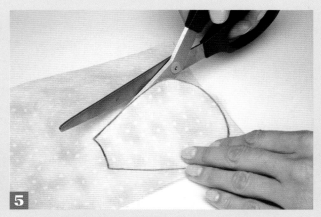

5

Remove the template from the fabric, and cut out the fabric piece along the marked line.

ironing recommendations

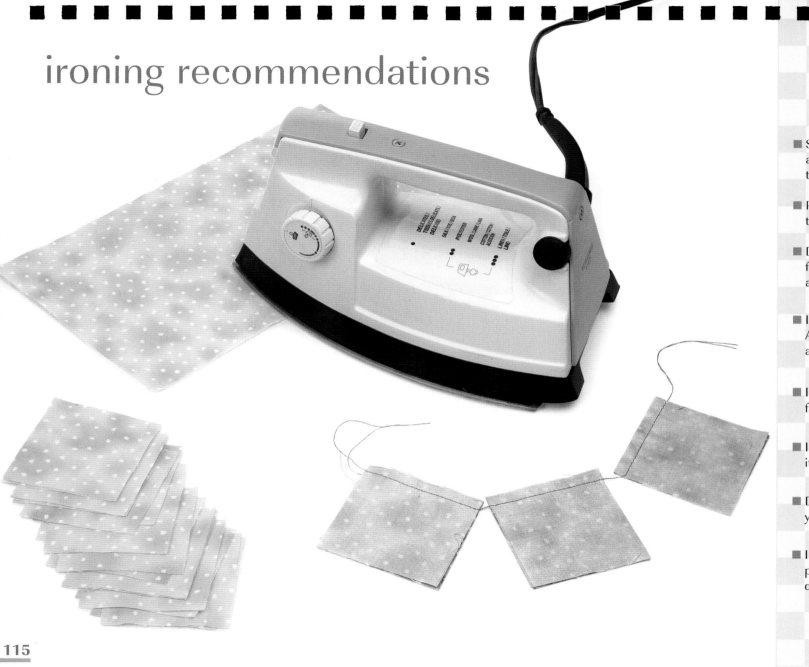

- Set the iron temperature according to the fiber content of the fabric you are ironing.

- Press the iron down firmly on the fabric; then lift it up.

- Do not slide the iron over the fabric, especially over seams, to avoid stretching the fabric.

- Iron each fabric unit as you sew. Avoid making any small folds along the seam line.

- Iron all seams toward the darker fabric.

- Iron the seam before crossing it with another seam.

- Do not iron seams open unless you are directed to do so.

- Iron the seams of connecting pieces or rows in opposite directions.

measuring and cutting the backing

The backing of the quilt should be about 3 in. (7.62cm) larger on all sides than the top of the quilt. This extra fabric allows for "take up" or shifting that occurs during the quilting process.

1. Measure the length and the width of the quilt top, adding 6 in. (15.24cm) to each measurement.

2a. For a quilt top that measures up to 78-in.-wide (1.98m), cut two lengths of backing fabric, each equal to the length of the quilt plus 6-in. (15.24cm). Use scissors to trim off the selvages from each piece. Position and pin the pieces together with their right sides together and edges even. Sew one long side ⅜ in. (0.95cm) from the edge. Iron the seams to one side. Trim the backing to the correct size, adding 6 in. (15.24cm) for "take up" before cutting the fabric.

2b. For a quilt top that measures more than 78-in.-wide (1.98m), cut three lengths of the backing fabric, each equal to the width of the quilt plus 6 in. (15.24cm). Use scissors to trim off the selvages from each piece. Position, pin, and sew two pieces together, attaching the third piece to one side of the pair. Iron the seams to one side, and trim the backing to the correct size, adding 6 in. (15.24cm) for "take up" before cutting the fabric.

Batting

Batting is cut the same way as backing fabric. Choose batting according to the quilting method that you plan to use (and the manufacturer's instructions). For machine-quilting, use a low-loft cotton or a cotton/polyester blend. For hand quilting, choose a thin cotton batting. For pre-packaged batting, unfold it to let it "rest" for a few days.

measuring and cutting the borders

Directions for cutting border strips are included in the cutting instructions for each quilt.

All dimensions are given for cutting crosswise border strips. (If you wish to cut borders lengthwise, additional fabric may be required.)

Cut the borders about 2 in. (5.08cm) longer than the given measurement because the quilt's length may vary slightly according to the precision of your cutting and piecing.

To obtain the necessary length when piecing border strips, piece the strips diagonally if the fabric has an all-over print. Piece the strips horizontally if the fabric has a directional print such as a stripe or a plaid.

Gently iron the body of the quilt before adding borders to it.

1. To measure the fabric for the borders, take both the length and the width measurements of your quilt top, measuring across the center of the quilt in two or three places each. Determine the length required for the side borders by averaging the lengthwise measurements.

2. Cut two strips for the side borders to the required length, and pin them to opposite sides of the quilt, matching the ends and centers, easing any fullness. Sew on the borders, and iron them.

3. For the top and bottom borders, take the average of the two or three widthwise measurements, including the side borders to determine the width required, and cut two border strips to the required length. Pin the borders to the top and bottom of the quilt, matching ends and centers, easing any fullness. Sew on the borders, and iron them.

Note: If your quilt design includes border squares, you will need to accomodate their measurments when assessing the measurement of the borders for the top, bottom, and sides of the quilt. In principle, you can follow the directions for adding the side borders, sewing them to the quilt top first. Then measure your top and bottom borders, adding two corner blocks to the measurement.

layering the quilt

Note: If the quilt top needs to be pre-marked, such as for ornamental quilting, mark the design or the quilting lines on the quilt top before layering the quilt sections together.

1. Place the backing, wrong side up on a hard work surface, using masking tape to secure the edges of the backing. Do not stretch the fabric.
Note: For a very large quilt, anchor the backing to a carpet using T-pins.

2. Center the batting on top of the backing, and smooth it in place.

3. Center the quilt top right side up on the batting, and smooth it in place.

Hand Quilting the Quilt Layers
Place the center of the quilt in a hoop or a frame. Begin quilting in the center of the quilt, working toward the outer edges.

1. Thread a size 8 "Between" needle with an 18-to-20-in.-length (45.72cm-to-50.8cm) of thread. Knot one end. Insert the needle into the quilt top and the batting,

being careful not to go through to the backing.

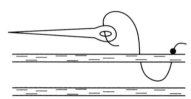

2. Pull the thread taut until it "pops" through the top fabric and into the batting.

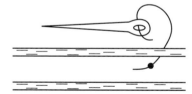

3. Put on a thimble. and hold the threaded needle in that hand. Place your other hand under the quilt. Push the tip of the needle down through all the quilt layers. When it touches your finger underneath, bring the needle back up through all of the layers, and

make 3–4 evenly-spaced stitches by rocking the needle up and down. Pull the needle and thread through the layers. Continue to hand-quilt as desired.

methods of quilting

Quilting is a process where neat, evenly-spaced stitches are used to hold the layers (top, batting, and backing) of the quilt together simultaneously producing simple or ornamental designs. Quilting can be done either by hand or by machine.

There are several types of quilting:

In the Ditch

Stitches are sewn on or close to the seam line ("the ditch") using monofilament or matching thread. The design does not need to be marked.

Outline

Stitches are made ¼-in. (0.64cm) from the seam line and can be marked. Outline stitches can be done "by eye" or guided by ¼-in.-wide (0.64cm) masking tape.

Ornamental

Stitches that are more ornamental in nature, such as curves and curlicues, are marked on the quilt top before the quilt is layered together.
Note: There is a wide variety of pre-cut quilting stencils and patterns that make the ornamental designs easy to transfer.

Marking the Quilt

Marking the quilt top can be done using fabric-marking pencils, a chalk marker, and white or silver pencils. Highly recommended are fabric-marking pens with ink that disappears when exposed to air or cold water. Also, when choosing a method of quilting, consider whether your fabrics are light or dark in color and whether your quilt top will be handled a lot during the quilting process.

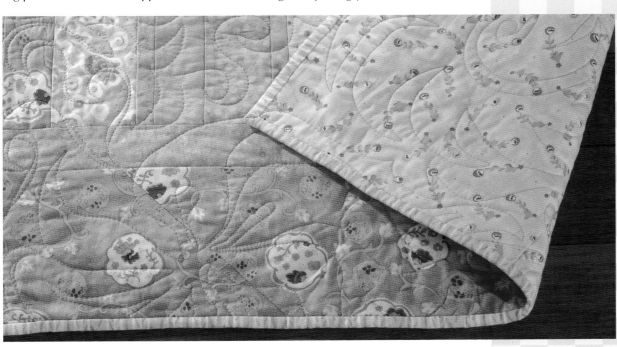

TIP

Patterns marked in chalk can rub off if the quilt is handled a lot, especially on those with intricate patterns. Choose a more permanent method.

machine-quilting

Machine-quilting is used on all the quilts in "The Collection." It is easy to do. You will need a sewing machine equipped with a special presser foot.

Choosing a presser foot:
If you are quilting straight lines, use a walking or even-feed presser foot to help the layers feed evenly through the sewing machine. For curved lines, such as those used in ornamental quilting, use a darning or machine-embroidery presser foot for free-motion quilting, and disengage the feed-dogs.

Choosing thread:
While thread color is always a matter of personal taste, thread should match the fiber of the fabrics being sewn. For thread that will be seen on the top of the quilt, load the top spool holder with monofilament or thread that matches the color of the top of the quilt. For thread that will be seen on the underside of the quilt, load the bobbin with monofilament or thread that matches the color of the quilt back.

Securing the thread:
Set the stitch width on your sewing machine to extra-short stitches. Sew a ¼-in. (0.64cm) line of stitches, then reset the stitch width as directed to continue machine-quilting.

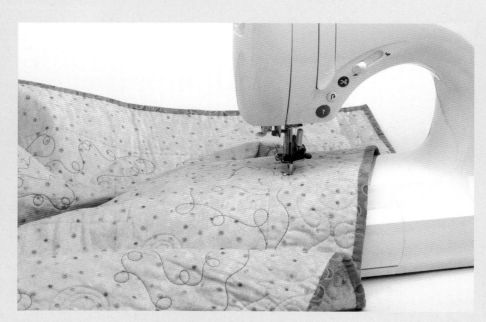

Machine-quilting using the "free-motion" method

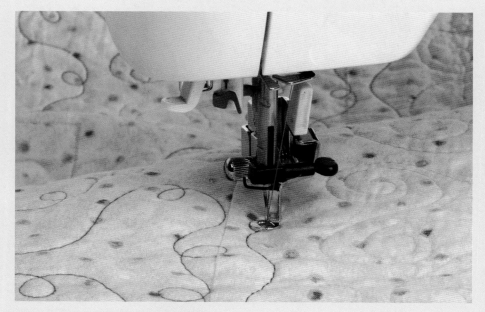

Detail of machine-quilted stitches

caring for your quilt

Washing

New quilts made of cotton and synthetics can be gently laundered. Fill a top-loading washing machine with warm water, and add a mild quilt detergent. Turn off the machine, and immerse the quilt. Soak the quilt for 5 to 10 minutes, agitating the fabric by hand. At the allotted time, drain the machine, refill it with warm water, and repeat the steps several times more until all the detergent has been rinsed out of the quilt. Use the spin cycle on your machine to remove the excess water. Then remove the quilt, and lay it on a flat surface, shaping it as necessary. When the quilt is nearly dry, air-fluff it in a dryer.

Freshening

To refresh your quilt and remove dust, air-fluff the quilt in a dryer.

Storing

Use a new, pre-washed white pillow-case, or wrap the quilt in plain muslin or acid-free tissue paper.

Never store your quilt in plastic.

If your quilt is folded and stored, refold it frequently in a different way to avoid wearing the folded edges.

Displaying

Never display your quilt in direct sunlight unless you want to fade the colors.

Hang your quilt from a sleeve of fabric sewn to the back of the quilt, and slip in a rod to keep the quilt from sagging.

Making a Label

Labels help identify the quilter and the quilt for future generations. Add any details you wish.

sources and resources

USA

Avlyn Inc.
1628 West Williams Drive
Phoenix, AZ 85027
623-209-2088
www.avlyn.com
*Designs and manufactures fabrics
specifically for quilters*

Benartex Inc.
1359 Broadway, Suite 1100
New York, NY 10018
212-840-3250
www.benartex.com
*Supplies designer cotton prints for
quilting*

Camelot Cottons
9600 Boul. St. Laurent, Suite 602
Montreal Quebec H2N 1R2
800-361-4120
www.camelotcottons.com
*Designs and manufactures fabrics
specifically for quilters*

FreeSpirit
1350 Broadway, 21st Floor
New York, NY 10018
212-279-0888
www.freespiritfabric.com
Manufactures designer cotton

prints for quilting

Hoffman Originals
4448 Winners Circle
Rocklin, CA 95677
916-624-1962
www.hoffmanfabrics.com
*Designs and manufactures
fabrics*

In the Beginning Fabrics
8201 Lake City Way NE
Seattle, WA 98115
206-526-6056
www.inthebeginningfabrics.com
*Designs and manufactures
fabrics*

LakeHouse Dry Goods
P.O. Box 162
Sterling Forest, NY 10979
845-595-6420
www.lakehousedrygoods.com
*Manufactures designer cotton
fabrics*

Moda Fabrics
13800 Hutton Drive
Dallas, TX 75234
972-484-8901
www.unitednotions.com
Manufactures fabrics, notions,

*patterns, books, quilting supplies,
and finished products*

P & B Textiles
1580 Gilbreth Road
Burlingame, CA 94010
800-852-2327
www.pbtextiles.com
*Designs and manufactures
fabrics*

**Quilting Treasures by
Cranston**
2 Worcester Road
Webster, MA 01570
800-876-2756
www.cranstonvillage.com
*Designs and manufactures
fabrics*

South Sea Imports
350 West Apra Street
Compton, CA 90220
310-763-3800
www.southseaimports.com
*Designs and manufactures
cotton fabrics specifically
for quilters*

Windham Fabrics
812 Jersey Avenue
Jersey City, NJ 07310

201-659-0444
www.windhamfabrics.com
*Designs and manufactures
fabrics specifically for quilters*

INTERNATIONAL

Cottage Quilting
2210 Highway 3B, Box 874
Fruitvale, BC V0G 1L0 Canada
250-367-9602
www.cottagequiltingonline.com
Sells quilting supplies and fabrics

The Cotton Patch
1285 Stratford Road
Hall Green, Birmingham B28 9AJ
+44 (0)121 702 2840
www.cottonpatch.net
*Sells quilting products, specializing
in patchwork*

Monika Carrie Design
West Haybogs
Tough / Alford
Aberdeenshire AB33 8DU
Scotland UK
+44 (0)197 556 2783
www.quilting-and-stitching.co.uk
*Sells patchwork, quilting, and
embroidery supplies*

acknowledgments

QUILT STYLE:
Cool and Cozy Coverlets
It may be my name on the door at Tammy Tadd Designs, but there are many people who make it possible for me to do what I do. Accordingly, I would like to try to give credit where credit is due.

For any talent that I might possess, all credit goes to my Heavenly Father. I am thankful that He created me just the way I am: an emotional, artistic female.

I so appreciate having the parents that I did. From day one, my mom, Velda, has been by my side. My dad, Roy, had such a great sense of humor. I believe that my parents' greatest gift to me has been their example of unconditional love for each other and their children. I will never take that for granted.

I am most thankful for and appreciative of my family. Gary, you have endeavored to support me at every turn—financially, spiritually, and physically. You have enabled me to do things in this lifetime that I would have never dreamed possible. Olivia, Stephanie, Nicholas, Haley, and Garrison—my wonderful, beautiful children—each one of you brings me such joy. You make me feel like the greatest mom in the world. Thanks for listening to my latest quilting news and pretending to be interested. Nick, thanks for your help and hard work at our shows, and for sporting the green apron and pink scarf!

What could be better in life than to do something you love every day with people who are not only the best employees in the world, but also some of your dearest friends. To each of them, a heartfelt thank you. Sherry and Dianna, you are both such blessings in my life; thank you for your friendship, hard work, fun-loving spirits, and for sharing yourselves and your families with me during all of these years.

Also, in the past year, we have had many other helpers in the studio as we have worked on this project. Sharon, thank you for your sweet spirit and your willingness to pitch in and do whatever was necessary. Sandy, you gave me such peace of mind; thanks so much for all of your help and creative ideas. Cindy, thank you for your "new-quilter excitement," and always being willing to try anything once; your faith inspires me. Rosie, my "Best Bud," thanks for being so willing to jump in and do anything I needed. You know the true meaning of friendship. Mary Lynn, thank you for always having a plan; thanks for researching, scheduling, and planning whenever I needed you to. God has blessed me with your friendship.

Thank you to Cranston Printworks Company and Kathleen Hill, Merchandising Manager, for contributing fabric from the Pink Ribbon Signature Collection by Karen Neuburger® ©2005 Quilting Treasures™ by Cranston®.

And last, but certainly not least, thank you to everyone at Creative Homeowner for their behind-the-scenes efforts in bringing to life the concepts you see in *Quilt Style*. A special thanks to Senior Editor Carol Endler Sterbenz, who for well over a year patiently communicated with me and assured me during each step in the process; thank you for your kindness and professionalism. Also, thank you to designer Glee Barre for contributing her unique vision and style to each beautiful page of *Quilt Style*. Special thanks also to the very talented and tireless photo team who brought the quilts to life. Thank you to photographers Steven Mays and Dennis Johnson and stylist Genevieve A. Sterbenz. A special thanks go to those friends in Huntington, NY, who opened their doors so graciously to the "invasion": Mary and Bernie Wytko, Mary Stokkers and Bob Hahn, Pam and Stan Gale, and Jean and Kent Gale. Your warmth and generosity are greatly appreciated.

index

If you like **Quilt Style** take a look at the other titles in our **Style Series**

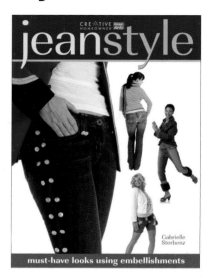